Christmas Angels

Christmas Angels

Phyllis Méras
Julianna Turkevich

Drawings by Julianna Turkevich

Houghton Mifflin Company Boston   1979

Library of Congress Cataloging in Publication Data

Méras, Phyllis.
  Christmas angels.

  1. Christmas decorations.   2. Christmas cookery.
3. Angels.   I. Turkevich, Julianna, joint author.
II. Title.
TT900.C4M47   745.59′41   79-15474
ISBN 0-395-27601-2
ISBN 0-395-28426-0 pbk.

Printed in the United States of America

M 10 9 8 7 6 5 4 3 2

Book design by Dianne Smith Schaefer, Designworks, Inc.

For Elisabeth and Nicholas Turkevich

Acknowledgments

We are grateful to many for their help in the preparation of this book, especially to Edward E. Goodwin and Alison Shaw for their photography; to Alan Berens of Carlisle, Massachusetts, for comfort and support; HSS, Inc., of Bedford, Massachusetts, for the use of its facilities; and to Linda Glick and Frances Tenenbaum for their editorial enthusiasm.

Rich in ideas and generous in their hospitality have been Susan Sirkis, Bettyanne Twigg, and Patricia Zipprodt. Also helpful have been George Adams, Janice Belisle, Virginia Blakesley, Candace Boyden, Stanley Burnshaw, Dennis Caprio, Peter Barry Chowka, Henry Cosimini, June Curme, Jane Farrow, Barbara Fitzgerald, Jean Fontenot, Josephine Golding, Gyda Gundersen Scandinavian Imports (of Cotuit, Massachusetts), Jeannette Hargroves, Georgette Hilliard, Margery Hilner, Janice Hull, Dorothy Kelly, Mary Mathews, Shirley Mayhew, Jeanne McCormack, Robert F. McCrystal, David Murphy, Ruth Nerney, Domer Ridings, Ruth Roberts, Esther Sellers, Margaret Schwankl, Jacqueline Smith and Faith Pierce (of the Providence [Rhode Island] Public Library), Thomas D. Stevens, Trudy Taylor, Eleanor Tinker, Travis Tuck, John E. Wallace, Linda Wrade, the Campbell Folk School (of Brasstown, North Carolina), and the Southern Highlands Handicraft Guild.

✿ Contents

❧ Introduction

IT IS CHRISTMAS EVE. I am sitting in the village of West Tisbury, Massachusetts, in a country house named God's Pocket. There is an array of angels on the cherry mantelpiece beside me.

There are crisp Scandinavian straw angels, gleaming copper angels, snowy-white angels carved from the wood of the holly tree, feather angels, clothespin angels, tissue-paper angels, bread-dough angels that were fashioned with artistry by Julianna Turkevich, the co-author and illustrator of this book.

We talk on the telephone, she and I — I on the island of Martha's Vineyard, she in Carlisle, Massachusetts. In her home, too, this Christmas Eve there is an assemblage of heavenly beings visiting here on earth.

What are angels? We have often asked each other this during this year of cutting and pasting and sewing of angels — and some of the things we learned surprised and delighted us.

Angels are neither a Christian nor a Jewish concept. There were angels in the religions of the Greeks and Egyptians, the Persians and Mesopotamians. Hermes, who had winged feet, was an "angeli," the Greek word meaning a messenger of the gods. When the religion of Zoroaster developed in Persia, there was one god, but with six associate spirits.

Angels, in most faiths, are said to emanate from God. Some say that these celestial beings are made from the fire that burns under the throne of God. That is why they glow. That is why there are myths suggesting that the stars are angels.

In the Jewish and Christian faiths, angels were largely created to praise God — the reason they are so often depicted singing or playing musical instruments. But angels are guardians, guides, counselors, matchmakers, and cooks, too.

It was an angel who rescued Daniel from the den of lions and Peter from prison. Angels warned Lot to leave Sodom before God destroyed it. Angels told the aged Abraham that Sarah, his wife, would conceive and bear a child who would be a leader of the Hebrew nation. Angels announced the birth of Christ. Angels were at the empty tomb when Christ rose from the dead.

Angels, in religion, are powerful creatures. In Gustav Davidson's *Dictionary of Angels* he notes that Gabriel was strong enough to carry Abraham on his back and the archangel Michael strong enough to lift mountains.

According to fourteenth-century estimates, there are more than 300,000,000 angels. In addition to their numbers, there is quite a hierarchy of angels (they are arranged in choirs).

There are seraphim, cherubim, and thrones; dominations, virtues, and powers; principalities, archangels, and angels, in descending order. Seraphim are the angels of love and light; the cherubim with flaming swords guarded the Garden of Eden. Dominations rule the other angels; virtues perform miracles on earth. Powers guard against the demons, who themselves are fallen angels. Principalities protect religion. Archangels are messengers to mankind, and just plain angels are concerned with individual people.

Initially, angels were sexless. Their wings (the seraphim were said to have six) may have originated because, being emanations of God, they glowed so brightly that they needed something to cover themselves so humans could look at them without being blinded. Their halos, too, were a result of the light that flowed around them. Wings, of course, sped them on their way between Heaven and Earth.

Until the fifteenth century, angels were an extremely important part of Christianity and were awesome creatures. Then they began to soften a bit in art and literature. In the early Renaissance, the cherubim with flaming swords became the sweet-faced cherubs playing with the Christ Child. And after the Renaissance, the woman's form began to appear among angels.

Today's angels — and most of the angels you will be making from the directions and plans in this book — are pretty, pleasant angels, kindly of expression. They are the angels beloved of the more than 250 members of the

American Society of Angel Collectors. They are the angels of Christmas cards and calendars. They are the angels to gleam from the top of your tree, to dangle in your window, to add to boxes of holiday cookies.

Down the road tonight, I see the dancing lights of a neighbor's Christmas tree in a front yard. It is homey and welcoming. That is what the angels on the mantel in God's Pocket are, too. They are just the kind God might well have tucked into his pocket to bring joy on Christmas Eve.

Phyllis Méras

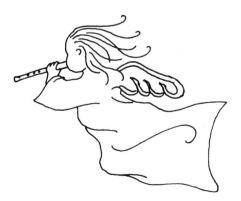

Christmas Angels

For he shall give his angels charge over thee, to keep thee in all thy ways.

They shall bear thee up in their hands, lest thou dash thy foot against a stone.

Psalms 91:11–12

Photo by Edward E. Goodwin

🌿 Origami angel

This tree-ornament–sized angel (4½ inches tall) is made from plain white paper and pieced with white glue. The only skill required is a good hand with scissors. Use any paper that has enough body to hold its shape after cutting and is easily cut with a pair of sharp scissors. Typing paper works well.

Tools and materials

one piece of white paper, 6 x 6 inches
a pencil, No. 3
spring clothespin
Elmer's Glue-All
sharp scissors
white thread or thin decorative cord for hanging

Finished size: 4½ inches high

Assembly

1. Transfer the outlines of angel pieces to the wrong side of the paper, using a No. 3 pencil. Angel parts are presented here to make a left-facing angel. Reverse the direction for a right-facing angel.

2. Cut on dotted lines around each piece before cutting out the actual piece. When cutting the pieces, take long cuts, using the entire length of the scissor blades, and turn the paper rather than the scissors for a smooth cut. When cutting out the halo, cut the inner curve first.

3. Cut the hair detail by beginning at the bottom back of the hair and making long curved parallel cuts toward the crown of the head. End these cuts at varying distances from the bottom for a natural look.

4. Fold the skirt lengthwise, like a fan, making ¼-inch folds. Folds should be slightly wider at the bottom than at the top. Twist the top of the skirt, and press it to make a flat surface. Put a few small drops of glue between the folds at the top and clamp the top of the skirt with a clothespin until the glue is dry.

5. Assemble the pieces with glue as directed below. Be careful to use small amounts of glue so the paper does not wrinkle. Do not get any glue on the front of the angel. A toothpick works well for applying small dots of glue.

   a. Attach the arm-and-horn section to the back side of the yoke. Before the glue has set, position the head behind the yoke section, placing the face so the horn mouthpiece is lapped behind it. Secure with glue and let dry.

   b. Place the hair over the head and glue the unstranded (top) part to the head. Use the picture as a placement guide.

   c. Glue the top of the skirt to the back of the yoke. Let it dry.

   d. Glue the wing to the back of the yoke.

   e. Glue the halo to the back of the head.

6. Leave the angel white or spray it with gold or silver paint.

7. Glue a 5-inch loop of white thread or decorative cording to the back of the angel for hanging. Secure this loop at the top of the skirt in back.

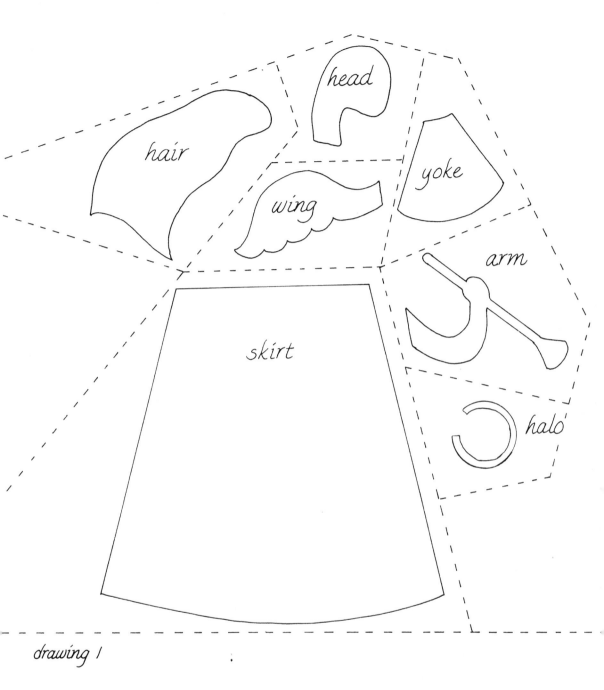

hair

head

yoke

wing

arm

skirt

halo

drawing 1

❧ Pine cone angel I

Photo by Peter Barry Chowka

Tools and materials

loblolly, slash, or longleaf pine cone
one Styrofoam ball, 1 inch in diameter
one 5- to 6-inch cardboard cone (you can make your own from
    an index card, stapling the sides together)
hemlock cones or small seeds
cornhusk
scissors
Bond-Grip glue
a strip of sycamore or birch bark, or wood-grained Con-Tact
    paper
cardboard for wings
3M Scotch Super Strength Adhesive Tape
acrylic paints
clear acrylic spray

Assembly

1. Pull the petals off the cone and glue them, seed side down, in a strip along the bottom edge of the adhesive tape. Attach the top half of the tape to the cone.

2. Soak the cornhusk in warm water for ten minutes. Then glue it, skin tight, around the Styrofoam head. Let it dry and paint on a face with acrylics. Glue on a halo of little hemlock cones or of seeds.

3. Glue the head to the top of the cone.

4. Cut wings 5½ inches long by 4 inches wide at the widest point.

5. Glue the birch or sycamore bark or the Con-Tact paper to the backs of the wings.

6. With adhesive, glue more cone petals to the front of the wings.

7. Let the angel dry. Then spray-paint it with clear acrylic spray.

Photo by Edward E. Goodwin

🌺 Claybake angel

Claybake dough is a wonderful medium — it is easy to make and work with, inexpensive, and delightful to all ages. Here is a claybake angel that is made simply by overlapping several basic shapes and adding a few decorative touches. After baking, it may be painted or left its natural golden-brown color.

Ingredients for claybake dough

4 cups white flour
1 cup salt
1½ cups water

fig. 1

Mix the flour, water, and salt thoroughly. Knead the mixture for several minutes, until it is elastic and smooth.

Refrigerate the dough until you are ready to use it, storing it in an airtight container. While you are working on the angels, keep the unused portion tightly wrapped.

While you construct the angel, work on a floured surface, directly on a baking sheet, or on aluminum foil. This will ease the transfer of the angel to the oven.

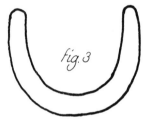

fig. 2

Tools and materials

claybake dough
aluminum foil or baking sheet
table knife
needle
toothpicks
rolling pin
pastry brush
acrylic paint
artists' paintbrush, medium size
Liquitex acrylic gloss polymer medium
colored string or gold-bead wire for hanging angel

Finished size: 3½ inches

fig. 3

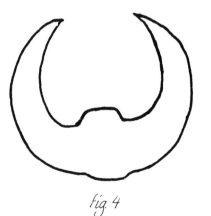

fig. 4

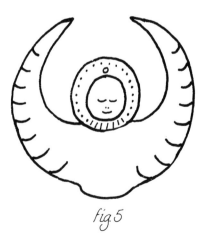

fig. 5

drawing 2

Assembly

Halo and head

1. Pinch off some dough about the size of a large pea. With your forefinger, flatten the dough into a circle 1 inch in diameter and 1/16 inch thick. This is the halo.

2. To the halo, add a smaller circle, thinner than the halo (*see Drawing 2, Figure 1*). Moisten the pieces of dough before you join them securely.

3. With a toothpick or needle, decorate the halo and draw an angelic face. Poke a hole all the way through the dough in the halo for hanging the angel (*see Drawing 2, Figure 2*).

Wings

1. Pinch off enough dough to make a roll 4 inches long and 1/4 inch in diameter. Shape the roll into a broad-based U shape (*Figure 3*).

2. With your fingertips or a rolling pin, flatten the U into a 1/16-inch thickness and form the wings (*Figure 4*).

3. Attach the halo/head to the wings. Add the wing detail with the sharp end of a needle, by gently drawing curved lines from the inner part of the wings outward (*Figure 5*). The lines should indent the dough smoothly and not produce a crumbly effect. Moisten the dough with a little water if necessary.

Body

1. Cut a dress shape (*Figure 6*), making the dough for the top part thinner than for the bottom.

2. Attach the dress to the halo/head/wing section, placing the dress over the wings. The top of the dress should abut the lower part of the halo.

3. Draw decorative lines along the bottom of the skirt, using a needle or a toothpick.

Arms

1. Make the arms by rolling a bit of dough, forming a U shape, and flattening it. Notch the center for the cuffs.

2. Transfer the arms to the angel; add hands if you want them (*Figure 7*).

fig. 6

fig 7

23

Baking

1. Bake the angel as soon as it is formed. The oven temperature should be 325–350 degrees. A counter-top toaster oven works well for small batches. If the angel puffs during baking, prick the puffs with a needle. The angel is done when it becomes firm and golden brown, which will take 20 minutes or more, depending upon the thickness of the dough. Check the underside to be sure the angel is done.

2. Cool the angel thoroughly before finishing it.

Finishing

1. Leave the angel its natural golden-brown color and seal both sides with varnish or clear enamel, *or*

2. Paint the angel with acrylic paint. When it is dry, give both sides of the angel a protective coat of acrylic gloss polymer medium.

3. Attach a hanging thread or wire to the hole in the halo.

Dough also lends itself to a more freeform angel. Use thinner pieces for the skirt and yoke of the angel's gown and drape them for a flowing effect. (Photo by Edward E. Goodwin)

There is a legend that the stars are angels, and another that the firefly is an angel looking for a lost love.

24

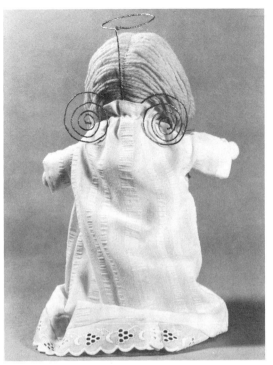

Photo by Edward E. Goodwin

Back view of angel hand puppet. (Photo by Edward E. Goodwin)

✤ Angel hand puppet

Tools and materials

pencil
one Styrofoam ball, 3 inches in diameter
one white tube sock, adult or teen size, plain knit (no cables or
      ribs), at least 16 inches long
scissors
white thread and needle
tailors' chalk
polyester fiberfill, approximately two thimblefuls, or cotton ball
yarn for hair, 50 strands of 14-inch lengths (about 20 yards)
pink embroidery thread (for facial features and for tying hair)
white cotton fabric, plain or with seersucker design, 2 pieces,
      each 12 x 12 inches
⅝-inch white eyelet trim, 26 inches long
covered florists' wire: one piece 28 inches long, one piece 14
      inches long
Testor's Pla enamel, gold
artists' paintbrush, No. 2 or 3

Finished size: 15 inches high

Assembly

Body

1. With the blunt end of a pencil, poke a hole in the Styrofoam ball 1¾ inches deep and wide enough for an adult middle finger (*see Drawing 3*).

2. Cut the tube sock off 12 inches from the toe (*see the cutting diagram, Drawing 4*). Turn the cut edge under 1 inch and hem. Save the remaining sock portion for arms.

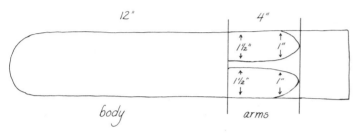

drawing 4

3. Insert the Styrofoam ball into the toe of the sock, with the hole pointing toward the sock opening. Stretch the sock smoothly over the ball; make sure any toe seam or manufacturer's marking is at the crown of the head and not on the face area.

4. Delineate the neck by gathering a line of basting stitches in the sock at the base of the ball (*see Drawing 5*). Use heavy-duty white thread or a double thickness of regular thread. When pulling up the basting stitches, leave enough space so a finger can fit through the sock and into the hole in the Styrofoam ball. Secure the thread temporarily; do not trim excess thread.

5. Lay the sock and ball on a flat surface, front side up. Lightly mark an F on the front chest area with tailors' chalk. Also on the front, with tailors' chalk or pencil, draw armhole slits 1½ inches long, beginning 1 inch below the neckline and indenting ⅜ of an inch from the sides of the sock (*see Drawing 6*).

6. Cut armhole slits through one thickness (the front) of the sock.

7. Gently loosen the neck basting, but do not remove it from the sock. Carefully slide the Styrofoam ball out of the sock.

Arms

1. Turn the remaining sock section inside out. Sketch arms as shown on the cutting diagram with pencil or chalk.

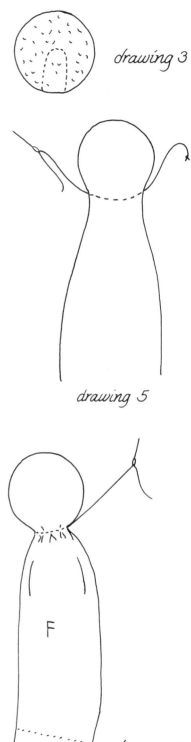

drawing 3

drawing 5

drawing 6

Make the arms 4 inches long and 1½ inches wide at the base, tapering to 1 inch at the hands.

2. With small stitches sew on the marked lines. Trim around the stitching, leaving ⅛-inch seams. Turn the arms right side out.

3. Turn the body inside out and insert the arms into the slits in the body. The right sides of the body and arms should face each other. Hand stitch with overcast, close stitches, using ¼-inch seams. Turn the body right side out.

4. Lightly stuff the hands with cotton or polyester fiberfill. Delineate the hands with a row of slightly gathered tiny stitches at the wrists (*see Drawing 7*).

Hair

1. Reinsert the Styrofoam ball. Position the finger hole correctly. Smooth the sock over the head and adjust any toe seam or marking. Pull up the neck thread and secure it permanently, leaving room for a finger. Trim the thread.

2. With a pencil or chalk, mark a line for the part on the head. Begin the front of the part about 2¾ inches above the front neckline and continue to 1 inch above the back neckline.

3. Starting at the forehead, position six strands, centering them on the part. Hold the strands securely between the index and third fingers of your non-sewing hand, as shown (*see Drawing 8*). Working from the forehead toward the back of the head, secure the yarn, one strand at a time, to the sock, on the part. Use a double strand of white thread and proceed as follows, using the sketch as a guide:

   a. Bring the needle up between the first and second strands.

   b. Insert the needle in front of the first strand; come out between the second and third strands.

   c. Insert the needle between the first and second strands; come out between the third and fourth strands.

   d. Insert the needle between the second and third strands; come out between the fourth and fifth strands. And so on.

When all the strands have been sewn into place, arrange the hair and trim to a uniform length if necessary. Divide strands at the base of the neck and secure each group with pink embroidery thread or ribbon.

drawing 7

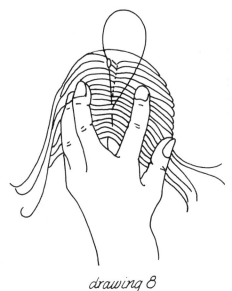

drawing 8

one square " 1 "

drawing 9

28

Face

Use rose-pink embroidery thread, a single strand, to give the angel eyes, nose, mouth, and cheeks. Use a stem stitch for the eyes and mouth and a satin stitch for the cheeks and nostrils.

Dress

1. On a piece of paper, 8½ x 11 inches, draw a 1-inch grid. Enlarge the dress pattern on the grid paper: one square on the pattern equals one square inch on paper (*see Drawing 9*).

2. Fold each piece of material in half. Place the fold of the pattern along the fold of the fabric and cut out. Repeat for the second piece of fabric. *Note:* You should now have two identical dress pieces, a front and a back.

3. Pin the front to the back, right sides together. Stitch together at the side seams and at the shoulders. Turn the dress right side out.

4. Apply trim to the bottom of the skirt; the seam for the trim should be at the center back.

5. Turn the neck edge under ¼ inch and hem it. Run a line of gathering stitches at the neckline ½ inch below the finished edge, but do not pull up the gathers at this time.

6. Put the dress on the doll by pulling the body down through the neck of the dress. Gather up the neck stitches and secure the thread, leaving clearance for a finger. Turn sleeves under to the desired length and hem with small stitches.

Halo and wings

1. For the halo, shape the 14-inch length of florists' wire as shown in Drawing 10. Use a small drinking glass (a cheese-spread jar is ideal) to shape the halo smoothly.

halo —
use 14" length of wire

drawing 10

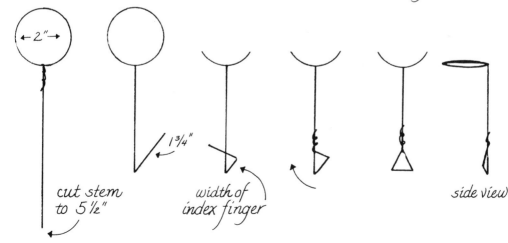

← 2" →

cut stem to 5½"

1¾"

width of index finger

side view

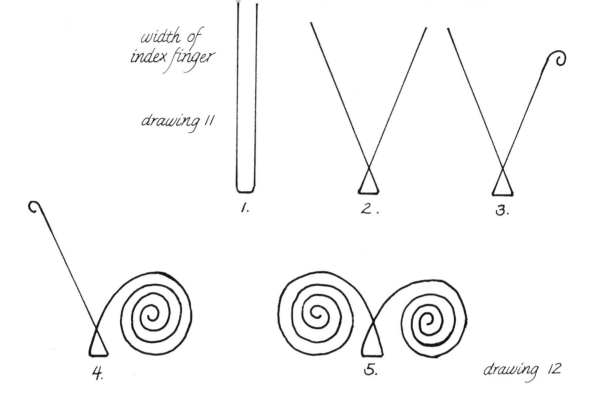

width of index finger

drawing 11

1.

2.

3.

4.

5.

drawing 12

wings - use 28" length of wire

2. For the wings, take the 28-inch length of florists' wire and bend it in the middle to form a U-shape, making the base of the U the width of your index finger, as in step 1 of Drawing 11. Shape the wings from the long stems of the U as shown in steps 2 and 3 of Drawing 11. The wings should lie flat when they are completed, as in steps 4 and 5 of Drawing 12.

3. Join the wings to the halo at the triangular bases with thread, as in step 6, Drawing 13. At this time, double check to be sure that the wings are flat (in line when you view them sideways) and that the halo is at a 90-degree angle to the halo stem and wings.

4. With an artists' paintbrush, paint the halo/wings gold. Hang by a thread from the triangular base to dry. Let the halo/wings dry completely.

5. When the halo/wings are *thoroughly* dry, slip the triangular base under the dress at the back of the neck. Secure the base to the sock with thread, using tiny stitches. Secure the halo stem to the part line with several tiny stitches. The halo should clear the head by ½ an inch.

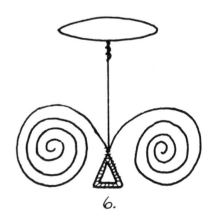

6.

drawing 13

 # Tin angel

Tools and materials

top and bottom of a large juice can
ruler
felt-tip pen
tin snips or heavy-duty scissors
breadboard or piece of plywood
needle-nosed pliers
a bead with a painted face (available in crafts-supply stores)
Elmer's Glue-All
glitter
gold braid
gold spray paint

Finished size: about 4 inches

Photo by Peter Barry Chowka

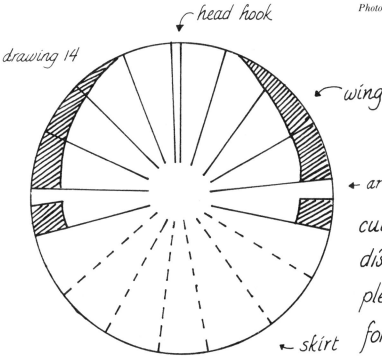

head hook

drawing 14

wing

arm

*cut solid lines
discard shaded areas
pleat dotted lines
for skirt*

skirt

Assembly

1. Lay the top of the juice can, top side up, on the breadboard or plywood. Using a ruler and a felt-tip pen, divide it into segments, following the pattern in Drawing 14.

2. Cut with the tin snips, following the pattern from the outer edge of the top to about ½ an inch from the center.

3. With the pliers, bend the arms in toward the center.

4. Also with the pliers, give a slight twist to each segment of the wings, so that they stand separate from each other.

5. Pleat the skirt with the pliers. Bend the last two pleats back to serve as a support for the angel when it stands. Decorate the skirt with glitter as you choose.

6. From the other end of the can, cut a small book shape. Punch two holes in it with the tin snips or scissors. Put the hands through the holes and bend them so that they hold the book.

7. Affix the bead head to the head hook.

8. Glue the gold braid hair to the head.

9. Spray the angel with gold spray paint.

Skirt is snipped, above; pleated, below. (Photos by Phyllis Méras)

Photo by Edward E. Goodwin

❧ Feather mobile angel

Tools and materials

one white drinking straw
scissors
yellow crochet cotton or six-strand embroidery floss, about
      12 inches long
long needle (at least 2¾ inches long) with large eye
Elmer's Glue-All
one ⅛-inch diameter wooden dowel, 5¼ inches long
three-sided file
two unpainted balls of balsa wood, ¾ of an inch in diameter, no
      holes
vise
hand or power drill with ⅛-inch drill bit
off-white quilting thread
eight clean white chicken feathers, at least 3 inches long
½-inch pine board scrap, unpainted, at least 4 inches long
hand or power plane
X-acto knife
white imitation feathers
a can or glass, 3½ to 4 inches in diameter

Finished size: 3½ inches high

33

Assembly

1. From the straw, cut two 2½-inch lengths for candles. Thread the long needle with the yellow cotton or floss and knot one end twice to make a large knot. Put a dab of glue on the knot and thread the floss through the straw; pull the knot into the straw about ¼ inch (*see Drawing 15*). Pinch the straw gently over the knot and hold it while you pull the floss at the other end and trim it to extend ⅛ of an inch beyond the end of the straw to make a flame. Make the second candle like the first. Set the candles aside.

2. Cut the wooden dowel to a length of 5¼ inches. Mark ¼ of an inch from each end and notch on the marks around the dowel with a three-sided file. Set the notched dowel aside.

3. Clamp the balsa balls in the vise. With a ⅛-inch drill bit, drill a hole through the center of each wooden ball. Pull an 8-inch length of white thread through each bead (*see Drawing 16*). Make a large knot in one end of each thread. Set the heads aside.

4. For each angel lay two chicken feathers together, one over the other. Clip the quills to a uniform length if necessary and insert the quills into the hole in the balsa ball. Secure the quills in the hole with glue and at the same time pull the white thread up so the knot is embedded in the glue and feathers (inside the ball). Set aside each set of feathers and head to dry. At this point the feathers should emerge from one end of the hole in the ball and the length of string should come out the other end (*see Drawing 17*).

5. Soak the 4-inch scrap of pine board at least eight hours.

6. Set the plane to cut about 1/64-inch shavings. Clamp the wood in the vise. Plane along the face grain of the wood to yield two strips about 4 inches long. These are arms. With an X-acto knife cut each strip to ½ x 3¾ inches. Cut one end of each strip at a slant, to simulate hands (*see Drawing 18*).

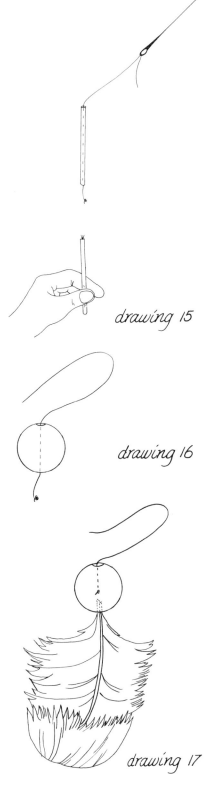

drawing 15

drawing 16

drawing 17

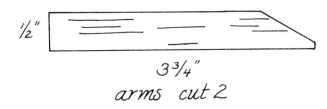

½"

3¾"

arms cut 2

drawing 18

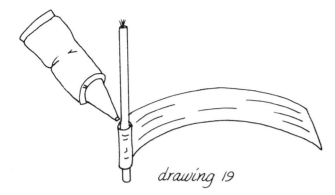

drawing 19

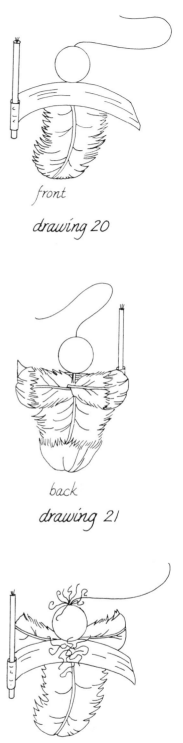

front

drawing 20

back

drawing 21

drawing 22

7. While the wood is still damp, curl it slightly, as shown, and wind the unbeveled end around a candle to form a hand. Have the candle extend below the hand about ¼ of an inch. As the arms face you, the candle should be on the left (*see Drawing 19*). Glue the hand around the candle with Elmer's glue.

8. Gently curve the arm around a can or glass (3½ to 4 inches in diameter, approximately) and make secure with a rubber band until the wood has dried.

9. Glue the arms onto the front of the feathers, abutting the head (*see Drawing 20*). Let the glue dry.

10. Take two of the remaining feathers and trim the quills to have a ¼-inch stub. Place one feather on each side of the angel's back so the feathers curve toward the back; secure the body feathers at the back with glue (*see Drawing 21*). Trim the wing tips to a uniform length, if necessary. Repeat for the second angel.

11. Put a small drop of glue into the hole at the top of the head and stuff a small amount of the imitation feathers into the hole with a toothpick. Make sure the hanging thread does not get caught and still comes out through the top of the head alongside the imitation feathers (*see Drawing 22*).

12. With small dabs of glue, attach the imitation feathers to the front of the angel at the center and at the center of the back between the wings, covering the glued places.

13. Attach the hanging thread of each angel to the notches at each end of the dowel. Adjust the lengths so the angels are 4 inches below the dowel, but do not cut off the excess thread at this time.

14. Double a 24-inch length of thread and tie in the center of the dowel.

15. Hang up the mobile and adjust the lengths of the supporting threads if the angels are not balanced.

✤ Copper angel for a tree

Tools and materials

one sheet of soft copper foil from a crafts-supply store
heavy-duty shears
cardboard
breadboard or piece of plywood
dull pencil
gloves
ticket punch or ice pick
ball-peen hammer

Assembly

1. Trace the pattern (*Drawing 23*) onto the cardboard.

Photos by Phyllis Méras

one square = 1"

drawing 23

2. Lay the copper foil flat on the breadboard or plywood. Trace the cardboard pattern onto the copper.

3. Cut the angel out of the copper.

4. Lay the angel back on the wood, and with the dull pencil draw on the facial features, wing feathers, and any design you wish to have on the robe. The figure will look better if some of the facial features (lips) and some of the decorative detail are drawn on the front and some on the reverse side of the copper. Should you wish to give a three-dimensional feeling to your angel, tape a cloth around a ball-peen hammer and do some hammering on the reverse side to create convex contours.

5. Punch a hole in the angel with a ticket punch or ice pick to hang it.

from The Marriage of Heaven and Hell

I have always found that Angels have the vanity to speak of themselves as the only wise; this they do with a confident insolence sprouting from systematic reasoning.

William Blake

Photo by Edward E. Goodwin

🌿 Pine cone angel II

Tools and materials

bow saw or coping saw with fine-toothed blade
one pine branch with bark, approximately ¾ of an inch in
    diameter and at least 8 inches long
one small pine cone, approximately 1 inch in diameter and at
    least 2 inches long
Elmer's Glue-All
one unpainted bead, ¾ of an inch in diameter with a ¼-inch
    hole
cardboard, 1½ x 1½ inches
gold lamé thread, approximately 2½ yards
scissors
artists' paintbrushes, No. 3 and No. 0
Testor's Pla enamel, brown, red, and gold
purchased gold wings with a wingspan approximately 3 inches
    wide by 1 inch high, or one 3 x 5-inch white index card

Finished size: 1¾ inches tall, with a wingspan of approximately
    3 inches

Assembly

1. With the saw, cut a diagonal slice from the pine branch (*see Drawing 24*). The slice should be ³⁄₁₆ of an inch thick and 2 inches long.

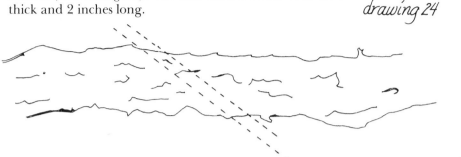

drawing 24

2. Turn the cone so the point is at the top (*see Drawing 25*) and break off the bottom portion, leaving a 1-inch length for the body of the angel.

3. Glue the cut side (scales pointed downward) of the cone into the center of the pine base, using Elmer's glue.

4. With Elmer's glue, attach the head to the top of the cone, fitting the pointed end of the cone into the hole. When the initial application of glue has dried, add several more drops through the top of the head to secure the bead well.

5. For hair, wrap gold lamé thread 25 times around a 1½ x 1½-inch piece of cardboard (*see Figure 1 of Drawing 26*).

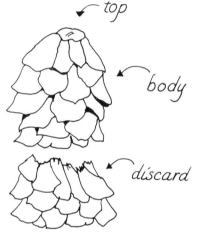

top

body

discard

drawing 25

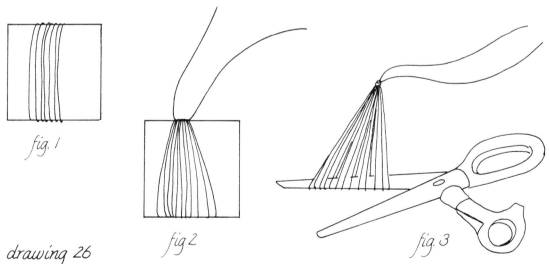

fig. 1

fig 2

fig. 3

drawing 26

6. With an additional 12 inches of gold thread, tie wrapped strands together at one edge of the cardboard, knotting the tie thread in its center (*see Figure 2*). Do not trim the tying thread.

7. Carefully slide the hair loops off the cardboard and cut the loops at the end opposite the tie (*see Figure 3*).

8. Determine which side of the angel will be the front (one side of the pine cone may be more uniform and pleasing than another). The front should be a lengthwise edge of the pine-branch base.

9. Apply small dots of Elmer's glue around the rim at the top of the head and position the hair on the head (*see Figure 1 of Drawing 27*).

10. Trim the bangs to ½ an inch below the tie, and glue the bangs to the forehead (*see Figure 2*). Secure the hair as well to the back of the head, but do not glue hair to the pine cone. Be careful not to glue down the hanging tie threads.

11. With the smaller paintbrush (No. 0), give the angel eyes and a mouth, using brown and red paint, respectively.

12. With the larger paintbrush (No. 3), accent the tips of the pine-cone scales with gold paint.

13. Cut the wings from an index card using the pattern provided (*see Drawing 28*), and paint both sides gold; or purchase the wings from a jewelry- or crafts-finding store.

14. Glue the center of the wings to the back of the pine cone, near the base.

15. Knot the two loose tie threads at the end to form a loop for hanging the angel (*see Drawing 28*).

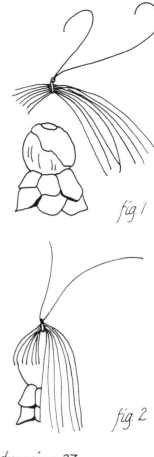

fig. 1

fig. 2

drawing 27

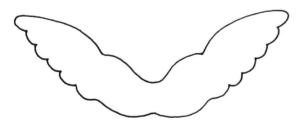

wing pattern

drawing 28

This carved wooden angel comes from Germany's Black Forest. (Photo by Edward E. Goodwin)

Papier-mâché angel

Tools and materials

22-ounce liquid detergent bottle
Yankee drill with second smallest drill bit
a package of 22–24-gauge copper wire
Sunday newspaper and a roll of paper towels
flour-and-water paste
foil pans for mixing paint and paste
strong scissors
fine sandpaper and an emery board
acrylic paints
artists' paintbrushes, including a fine one (No. 0) for facial
     details
a hank of yarn
a 2-foot-square piece of cotton cloth for the angel's robe
braid, sequins, gold leaf for trim
Duco cement
straight pins
cardboard or paper for cutting patterns
a strip of balsa wood, at least 2 feet long and 3 inches wide (from
     a hobby shop)
clean rags

Finished size: about 12 inches

Photo by George H. McAllister, Jr.

Assembly

1. Remove the cap from the bottle and set it aside where it will not get lost.

2. Now imagine that you are holding a figure of a headless and armless milkmaid. Drill two holes for the arms, one above the other, about ¼ of an inch apart, in each shoulder of the figure. Use the finest drill bit.

3. Turn the figure upside down and drill two holes where you think each leg would be attached to the torso. If you make a miscalculation, new holes can be drilled later.

4. To form each arm, take a piece of the wire, approximately 10 inches long, and make a hook at one end. Bend the wire and fashion a mitten-like hand in the middle. Bend both wire ends into right angles where they will enter the shoulder and insert them into the armholes you have drilled. Repeat for the other arm.

5. Using the newspaper, cut a pile of paper strips ¼- to ½-inch wide and no more than 4 inches long.

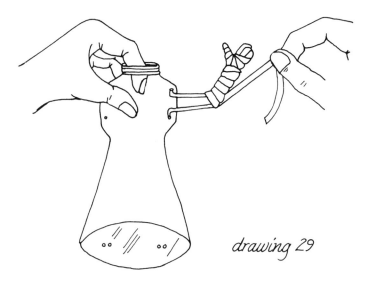

drawing 29

6. Mix the paste to a creamy consistency, but don't make any more than a cup at a time, for it hardens quickly.

7. Dip each strip into the paste. Smooth off the excess. Wrap one layer of strips around each wire arm. Let them dry. Apply a second layer, going in the opposite direction. Let it dry. Fatten the top of the arm, the upper back, shoulder, and chest with third or fourth layers. Wind the paper strips the way you wind an Ace bandage (*see Drawing 29*). You may need quite a lot of paper to give

44

shape to the arms, but be sure to let each layer dry thoroughly before you apply a new one. The top layer should be made of paper toweling rather than newspaper for it provides a better surface to paint.

8. To form the skull, turn the bottle cap upside down and glue it into the bottle's "neck" cavity. Fill the cap with more globs of paste-soaked paper strips put together in the shape of a skull (or egg). The head should be about 2 inches from top to bottom. Dry the head overnight.

9. In the morning, wrap the head and neck carefully in strips of the paste-soaked toweling. Smooth out the shape of the face. Push out a nose (an orange stick is a helpful tool for doing this). Let the head dry completely.

10. Turn the figure upside down and form the legs and feet, one at a time, using the same method used to form the arms. For each, use approximately 14 inches of wire. Dry the angel overnight on its head.

11. In the morning, sand the angel gently, using the emery board to get at small areas and fine curves. The angel may feather a little, but don't worry about it, for the paint you apply later will act as glue.

12. Mix a little burnt sienna paint with white acrylic until you have achieved the flesh tone you wish. Cover the arms, legs, and head with several coats (you may need up to four).

13. Cut yarn for the hair to the length you wish. Position it on the head with straight pins and then glue it on in sections. (Remember that most hair has a part.) Remove the pins before the hair is completely dry.

14. With the fine brush, paint the eyes and lips.

15. Using Drawing 30 as a guide and either cloth or paper as material, cut two bodice pieces and two sleeves.

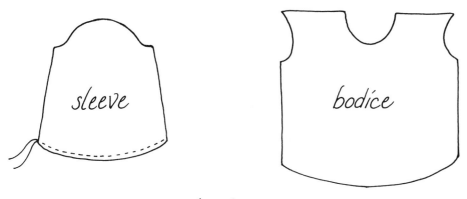

drawing 30

The back is 4 inches from shoulder to shoulder and 3½ inches in length. The sleeves should be 4½ inches from the top to the cuff and about 2 inches across at the cuff.

16. When you have cut out the sleeves, sew a drawstring into the cuff of each. Dip the sleeve gently into the paste and wrap it gently around the arm. Draw the string and let the sleeve dry. Repeat this procedure for the other arm.

17. Paint an extra layer of paste on each arm to make the sleeves stiff. Add as many coats of paste as you need, but let each dry before another is added.

18. Place the back of the bodice on the figure. Layer it with paste. Let it dry and put it on the front bodice. Paint it with paste. When it is dry, if you like, you might wish to add a collar, following the same procedure.

19. Sand the bodice gently and paint as you desire.

20. To make the skirt, pleat two pieces of newspaper, 9 inches long by 12 inches wide. Pin them to the waist. Cover the pins with a paper belt that you paste in place.

21. Coat the skirt and the belt with several layers of paste, again letting the material dry between coats.

22. When the angel is thoroughly dry, paint it as you wish, adding decorative details — yarn, braid, sequins.

23. Now cut two wing patterns out of the cardboard, using Drawing 31 as a guide. The wings should be about 9 inches long and 3 inches wide. Hold the wings behind the angel to see if they are a size that appeals to you. When they are as you like them, trace the pattern onto the balsa wood and cut it out with a sharp knife.

24. Sand the rough edges.

25. Paint both sides of the wings with several coats of acrylic paint to fill all the pores in the wood. Let the wings dry.

26. Pin the wings to the back of the angel.

27. In the flat section, on the inside of the wings, drill two holes, one above the other, about ¼ of an inch apart, being sure to penetrate both the wood and the bottle's back.

28. Remove the wings and paint them as you wish.

29. Thread a piece of wire through the holes in each wing and into the holes in the body to attach them securely, as in Drawing 32.

30. Dip the cotton fabric you plan to use for a robe into the paste. Smooth off the excess. Drape the robe over one shoulder of the angel and arrange it into folds. Pin it in place and remove the pins when the robe is dry.

31. Turn the figure over and drill two holes in the

wing

drawing 31

upper back between the wings. Cut a length of wire and loop it. Fork the ends and fit them into the holes so that you have a hanger. Tape the hanger in place for further security or stick the ends of it into the holes after they have been daubed in Duco cement.

32. Now draw a circle on the balsa wood that will make an appropriate halo. It should be about 2½ inches in diameter. Cut it out and sand it. Paint both sides with white acrylic. Let it dry. Then paint on the design you wish your halo to have. Or you might prefer simply to apply gold leaf. When the halo is dry, glue it to the back of the angel's head. Reinforce it by pushing three pins through it into the back of the head; the glue alone probably will not hold.

33. Draw a sickle shape with a tapered handle on a piece of cardboard. Then trace it onto the balsa wood. Cut, sand, and paint.

34. Drill a hole through the angel's right hand. Squeeze glue into it and insert some straw flowers. Glue the sickle into the hole, too, and then pin it in place temporarily. Remove the pin when the glue is dry.

back view

drawing 32

Photo by Edward E. Goodwin

Scandinavian felt angel

Tools and materials

felt, one 4 x 6-inch piece, in red, green, yellow, pink, et cetera
scissors
Scotch Rug-N-Carpet tape, 1¼ inches wide
⅟₃₂-inch balsa wood, 2 x 3 inches
X-acto knife
Elmer's Glue-All
two or three tiny dried flowers, with stems
waxed paper
heavy book (to be used as a weight)
gold beading wire, No. 34 size, about 8 inches
needle with large eye to accept beading wire
one ¾-inch or ⅝-inch unpainted wooden bead with hole
      approximately ¼ inch in diameter
yarn for hair: 6 or 7 strands of thick yarn (about ³⁄₁₆ inch in
      diameter)
Testor's Pla enamel, red, white, blue
artists' paintbrush, No. 0 or No. 1
embroidery thread compatible with dress color, about 8 inches
      long

Finished size: 3¼ inches tall

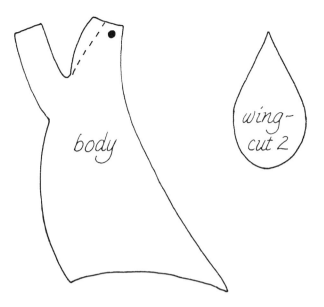

drawing 33

Assembly

1. Cut two wings from balsa wood by first placing the pattern (*follow Drawing 33*) over the wood and then tracing it with a pencil. This will leave an indentation in the wood that will serve as a cutting guide. Place the wood on a magazine to protect the working surface. Cut out the wings, using an X-acto knife.

2. Iron the felt and fold it in half to make a piece 3 x 4 inches. Cut along the fold.

3. On one piece of the felt, lay two 3½-inch lengths of carpet tape, side by side.

4. With chalk or pencil, trace the body pattern onto the other piece of felt.

5. Place the marked felt on top of the felt with tape, aligning the edges of the felt. The marked side of the felt should be up. Do not press the two pieces of felt together firmly.

6. With sharp scissors, cut out the body shape.

7. Carefully open the back seam of the body and insert the wings, slightly overlapping one another and extending about ¼ of an inch into the body. With a toothpick, add a couple of drops of glue between the felt and the wings. Press the felt firmly together at the wings.

8. Gently separate the ends of the arms and insert the stems of the dried flowers; secure with glue between the layers of felt. Press the arms firmly together.

49

9. Lay the angel on a flat surface and cover it with a piece of waxed paper. Weight the angel with a heavy book while you prepare the head. Do not crush the flowers with the book!

10. Thread a needle with an 8-inch length of gold beading wire and run the wire through the felt at the neck (refer to the dot on the pattern shown in *Drawing 34*). Remove the needle and twist the ends of the wire together at the neck.

11. Fold the neck toward the back as indicated by the dotted lines on the pattern. Pull the gold wire through the hole in the bead. Fit the folded neck into the hole and secure the head to the top of the neck with a dab of glue.

drawing 34

drawing 35

drawing 36

drawing 37

top view

drawing 38

drawing 39

12. Pull the wire to the forward edge of the hole in the top of the head (*see Drawing 35*). Loop the wire backward and then toward the front of the angel, as shown in Drawings 37 and 38. Apply small amounts of glue around the rim of the hole and position six or seven strands of yarn for the hair, covering the gold wire as it curves toward the front, as shown in Drawing 38. While the glue is still wet, pull up the gold wire to form a part for the hair (*see Drawing 39*). Carefully wipe off any glue which is on the ends of the wire.

13. Paint the face and give the angel pink cheeks (mix a dot of red paint into some white for pink).

14. Tie short lengths of embroidery thread around the strands of hair, as shown in the photograph.

Variation

Omit the yarn, and glue on a small cotton ball for the hair (first pull cotton gently to expand and shape), and give the angel a horn and a halo made from thin gold foil. The horn is 1⅜ inches long; glue it instead of the flowers between the ends of the arms. The halo is ¾ of an inch in diameter. After the hair is secured, knot the gold wire ⅛ of an inch above the angel's head; string the halo onto the wire (*see Drawing 40*) and knot the wire again to keep the halo in place.

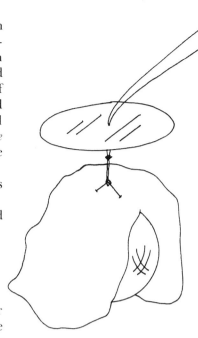

drawing 40

Simple angels like these may also be cut from felt. (Photo by Peter Barry Chowka)

❧ Cornhusk angel

Tools and materials

eight cornhusks:

      one 4 x 2 inches for the head
      one 6 x 2 inches for the arms
      four 7 x 4 inches for the dress
      one 4 x ½ inch for the wings
      one of any size, from which the halo will be cut
half a paper handkerchief
thin wire (or peeled sandwich-bag fastener)
raffia
scissors
Elmer's Glue-All
cornsilk or jute
one rounded toothpick
masking tape
India ink
straight pen
Rit dye

Finished size: 5 inches

Photo by Phyllis Méras

Assembly

    1. Dampen the cornhusks under the tap. If you want to dye the husks with Rit, follow the directions on the package, but leave them in the dye overnight for a rich color. Rinse and lay them out on newspapers to dry. Re-wet them before using.

    2. Lay the 4 x 2-inch husk flat on the table. Twist it in the middle until it is in a bow-tie shape, as in Drawing 41.

    3. Wad the paper-handkerchief half into a ball and lay it on one side of the bow tie (*see Drawing 42*).

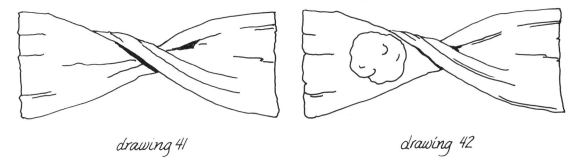

drawing 41

drawing 42

4. Fold the other half of the tie over so that the wadded handkerchief is completely covered, as shown in Drawing 43.

5. Tie a bit of raffia very tightly below the handkerchief (*see Drawing 44*), forming the angel's head. Set it aside, temporarily.

6. Lay the 2 x 2-inch husk out flat, rough side out. Lay the wire down the center of it, extending the wire about ½ an inch beyond the husk on each end. Roll the husk loosely around the wire (*Drawing 45*) to make the sleeves of the angel's dress.

7. Lay this arm piece below and behind the head. Starting with the raffia in back, tie the arm piece beneath the head, crossing the raffia in front, bringing it around in back again, and tying it tightly in back, in order to bring the arms forward, as shown in Drawing 46.

8. Fold the long edges of the 7 x 4-inch husks under about ½ an inch.

arms

drawing 45

drawing 43

drawing 44

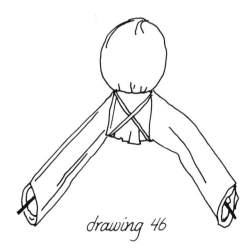

drawing 46

9. Holding the head and arm piece in one hand, with your other hand arrange the dress husk around the head, with the rough side and narrower end facing the head, as in Drawings 47 and 48. There should be about 1 inch of husk below the head.

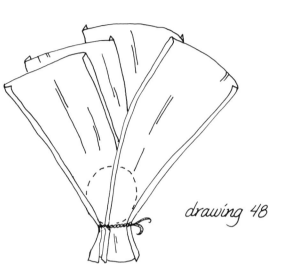

drawing 48

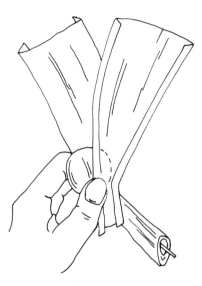

drawing 47

10. Tie a piece of the raffia tightly just below the neck. Then, as if you were peeling a banana, turn the husks down from the head to make a dress (see Drawing 49).

11. Tie another piece of raffia around the waist, knotting it in front. Cross the ends over the shoulders, tying them together in back to create a hanger for the angel.

12. Glue the bottom and sides of the dress together with Elmer's glue.

13. To achieve the flying effect, prop the angel up and press a book or other heavy object against the bottom of the skirt at an angle, leaving it until the angel is dry.

14. Bend and shape the arms.

15. Break the toothpick into thirds and wind two of the pieces in masking tape. Discard the center third and dip the pointed end of each remaining piece into the glue and insert the arms into the sleeves.

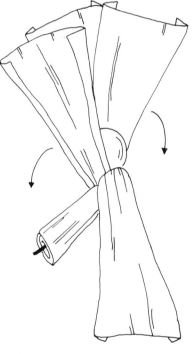

drawing 49

54

16. Cut simple wings out of the 4 x ½-inch husk. The wings should be tapered and about 2 inches long by ½ an inch wide at the widest point.

17. With raffia, sew the wings to the back of the angel.

18. Glue on cornsilk or jute for the hair.

19. Glue on a halo 1 to 1½ inches in diameter, dyed golden.

20. Paint on the features with India ink and a straight pen.

This standing cornhusk angel was designed by May Ritchie Deschamps of Swannanoa, North Carolina, whose cornhusk dolls have been exhibited at the Smithsonian Institution in Washington, D.C. (Photo by Peter Barry Chowka)

Photo by Edward E. Goodwin

🎄 Pleated paper angel

Materials

Reader's Digest (or Sears Roebuck catalogue or telephone book if
      you would like an angel doorstop)
small silver Christmas-tree ball
silicone glue
contact cement
one pipe cleaner
matte flat-finish spray paint
gold glitter

Assembly

    1. Close the magazine. Fold the top corner of the
cover down until it meets the spine, forming a triangle (*see
the second photograph*).

2. Fold the bottom corner of the cover up to meet the side of the triangle you have just folded. You should now have a large triangle made from the top of the cover page and a small one made from the bottom. Continue folding about a third of the magazine's pages in this way.

3. To make the wings, fold the lower corner of the next six pages up to meet the magazine's spine, and the upper corner of those pages down to meet the side of the lower triangle. These pages should have the large triangle at the bottom and the small one at the top.

4. Resume folding the remaining pages (all but the last six) as you folded the first pages with the large triangle at the top and the small one at the bottom.

5. Fold the last six pages with the large triangle at the bottom again and the small one at the top.

6. Spread the pages and stand the book up with the small triangle at the bottom. The bulk of the large triangles will then make the angel's dress, and, above it, you will see that you have wings.

7. With a wire cutter or old scissors, cut the pipe cleaner to the appropriate size for a halo. Using the contact cement, glue the halo to the Christmas ball, Let it dry.

8. Put a glob of silicone glue on top of the spread-out, standing figure. Glue the Christmas ball with its halo to it.

9. Spray with spray paint and sprinkle with gold glitter. When the figure is dry, you can add a sprig of holly to the angel's collar.

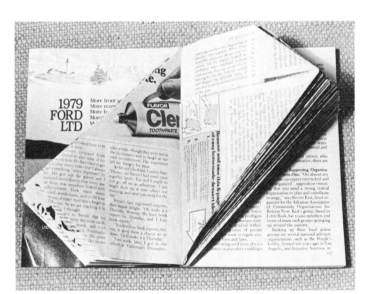

Photo by Phyllis Méras

Photo by Edward E. Goodwin

❧ Sachet angel

Tools and materials

unbleached muslin, ⅜ yard of 36-inch fabric
pencil or tailors' chalk
white or off-white thread
needle
straight pins
sewing machine (optional)
scissors
quilting thread
off-white lace trim, about ¾ inch wide, 1 yard long
polyester fiberfill
two long-haired synthetic fur scraps, 4 x 4 inches
Elmer's Glue-All
dried lavender leaves or potpourri, approximately 1 ounce
paper or large index cards

Finished size: approximately 7 inches high

Assembly

Head and body

1. Transfer the body pattern to a double thickness of muslin, using pencil or chalk to mark the fabric (*see Drawing 50*).

drawing 50

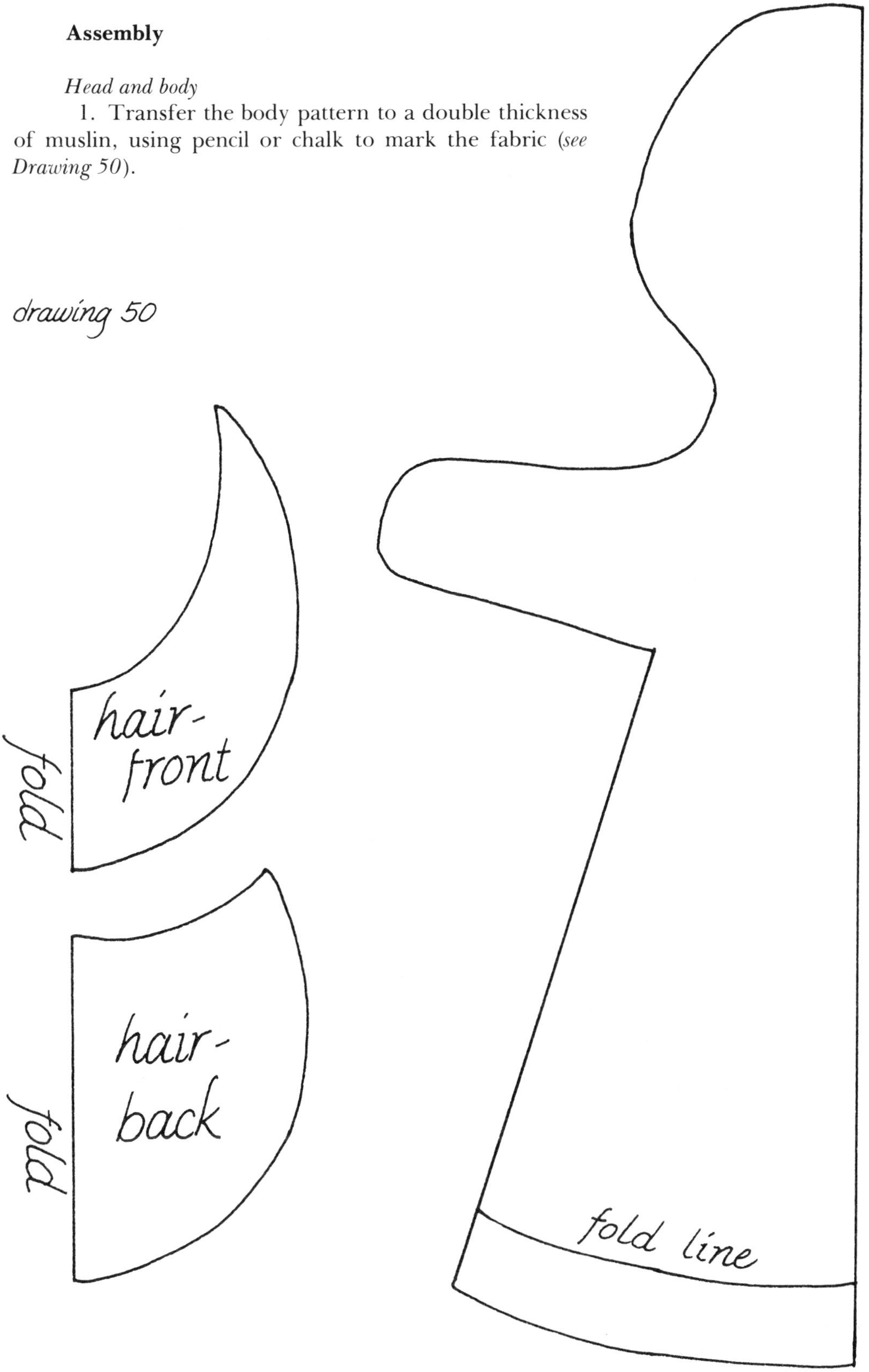

hair-
front

fold

hair-
back

fold

fold

fold line

2. Using small stitches, machine stitch the outline of the body through both thicknesses of muslin. Take care to stay directly on marking and to make smooth curves. Do not stitch across the bottom of the skirt.

3. Trim away excess fabric to ⅛ of an inch from the stitching, except at the bottom of the skirt. There, leave ½ an inch beyond the marked line. Clip the neck and underarm curves to the stitching (*see Drawing 51*).

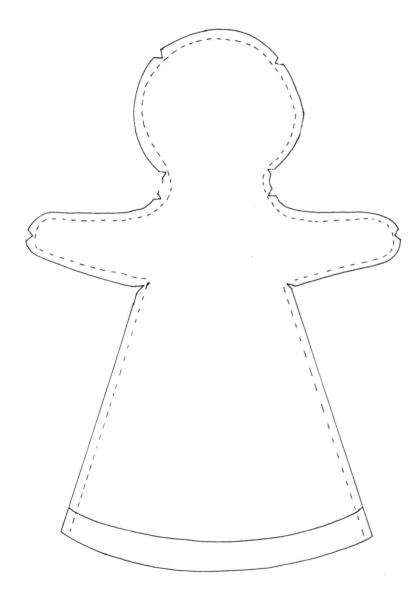

drawing 51

4. Turn the angel right side out. Turn the bottom skirt seam inside and press along the marked line.

5. Cut a length of lace to fit around the bottom edge of the skirt, with an extra ½ inch for a ¼-inch seam.

6. Place the lace along the outside of the skirt edge, overlapping the muslin ¼ of an inch. The ends of the lace should form a seam at one side of the skirt. Hand stitch the lace to the skirt with tiny stitches.

7. Stuff the angel's head and neck with fiberfill until very firm.

8. Stuff the arms with fiberfill; the stuffing here should be less firm than in the head, and the area where the heavy dotted lines are on the pattern should only have a thin layer of fiberfill.

9. Machine or hand stitch the angel on the heavy dotted lines near the arms.

10. Finish stuffing the doll with herbs (dried lavender, potpourri, et cetera). The body of the doll should be fairly firm.

11. Machine stitch the bottom edges of the skirt together, just below the lace/muslin seam. Make sure the bottom edges of the lace are even.

12. Run a double line of hand stitches under the chin and pull up tightly (see Drawing 52). This will cause the angel's head to bow forward. Knot the thread at the back of the head where it will be covered later with hair.

Wings

1. Cut one piece of muslin 4 x 12 inches.

2. Turn under ½ inch along each 12-inch edge of the wing piece and press.

3. Cut two 12½-inch lengths of lace and pin each along the right sides of the long edges of the muslin. The lace trim should overlap the muslin ¼ inch. Hand stitch the lace in place and trim the ends even with the muslin (see Drawing 53).

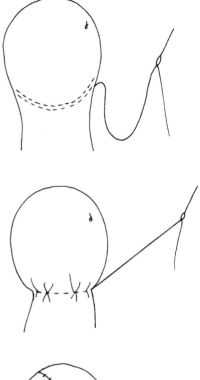

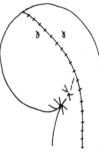

drawing 52

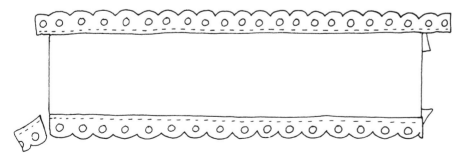

drawing 53

61

4. Machine stitch the two 4-inch edges of the wing piece to one another, right sides together, forming a tube.

5. Turn the wing section right side out and press, placing the seam in the center of the wing (*see Drawing 54*).

6. Lay the wing on the working surface, with lace edges at the top and bottom and the seam against the table. With both thicknesses of fabric, make three horizontal tucks at the center of the wing. The tucks should be about ¼ of an inch deep and will reduce the width of the wing at the center to approximately 1½ inches. Pin each tuck and machine stitch through all tucks (*see Drawing 55*). Do not stitch through the lace trim.

7. Position the wing to the angel, placing the top of the lace even with the neck (*see Drawing 56*). The seam side of the wing should be against the angel's back.

8. Stretch the wing to fit snugly across the angel's back (*see Drawing 56*). Stitch the wing to the body at the heavy dotted lines by the arms (*see Drawing 57*), sewing directly over the previous line of stitching.

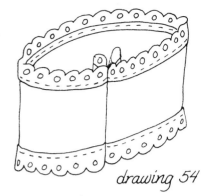

drawing 54

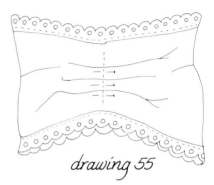

drawing 55

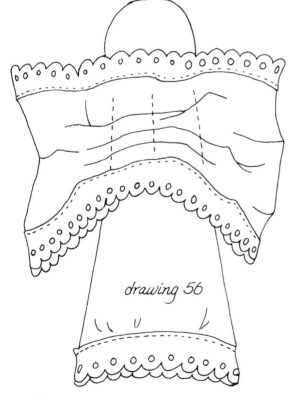

drawing 56

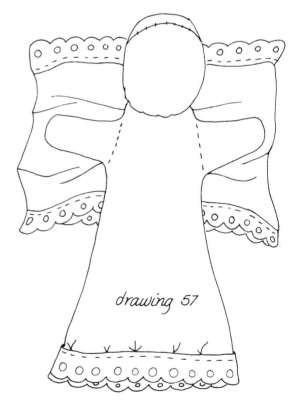

drawing 57

Hair

1. Fold two pieces of paper or large index cards in half. Place the patterns on the folds of paper to make templates for the front and back hair sections (*see Drawing 41*).

2. Trace each template onto a single thickness of synthetic fur. Cut one piece each front and back.

3. With hairy sides facing one another, stitch the outer curve of the hair sections together with a ¼-inch seam. Trim the seam and clip the curves so the pieces will turn well (*see Drawing 58*).

4. Turn the hair right side out, and fit it onto the angel's head. Tuck the pointed ends at the sides under and toward the back of the head. Secure the hair to the head with glue.

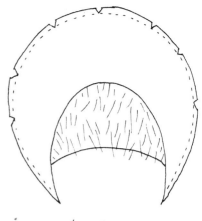

drawing 58

Finishing

1. Bring the angel's hands together and secure them with tiny hand stitches (*see Drawing 59*).

2. With a double strand of embroidery thread, give the angel blue or black eyes. Use a satin stitch.

3. Attach a loop of invisible fishing line or heavy white thread to the back of the wing or the top of the head.

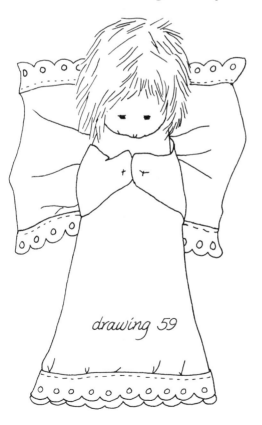

drawing 59

63

✿❊ Stained glass angel

Tools and materials

stained glass bought in a hobby shop (or old glass plates, saucers, et cetera, from a flea market)
cardboard
a glass cutter
pliers
single-channel lead came (from a hobby shop)
metal or nail clippers
ball-point pen
50–50 wire solder
soldering iron
flux
copper wire
picture wire
marble surface to work on

Finished size: 4½ inches

Photo by Phyllis Méras

Assembly

1. Draw a simple four-piece angel of the size you wish (or copy *Drawing 60*) onto the cardboard and cut out the pieces.
2. Lay the pieces on the glass. Scratch around the pattern outline with the glass cutter, being careful to scratch with just one stroke.
3. With the pliers, break off the glass outside your pattern pieces. If the edges are not smooth, they can be touched up later by gently rolling the pliers over the rough edges and chipping away.
4. Unroll the lead came and bend it around the edges of each separate piece of glass. Gently press it close to the glass with the pen. When the glass is outlined, cut off the end of the lead with the metal or nail clippers.
5. Apply a drop of the flux wherever the pieces of the angel will fit together — where the wing meets the body, the arms, the head, et cetera. Unroll a length of the spool of solder and, by holding the soldering iron close, melt the solder at the joint, but beware of having it too close too long or the lead will melt.
6. Solder the joints on both sides.

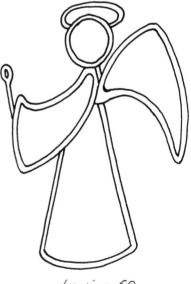

drawing 60

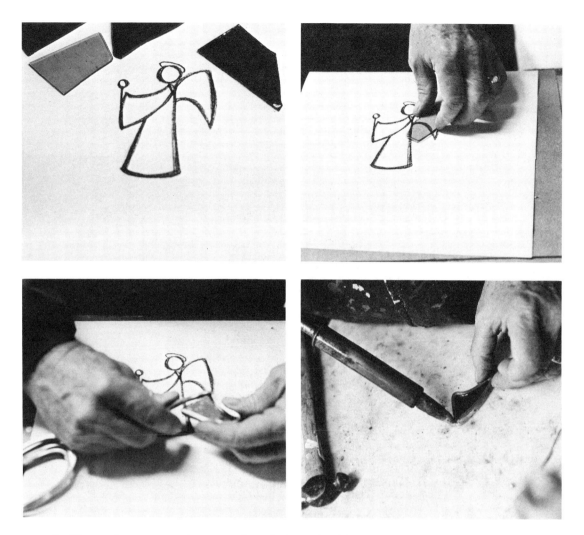

7. Shape the copper wire to make a halo and solder it onto both sides of the head. Again, beware of melting the lead.

8. When the solder has set firmly, tie a wire to the halo to dangle the angel in the light from a window, or on the Christmas tree.

9. Ajax will clean off any flux that remains on the glass.

Photos by Phyllis Méras

🌿 Quilted angel

Make several of these quilted angels and suspend them above your Christmas tree or Nativity scene. Alternatively, they make endearing dolls.

Tools and materials

graph paper with ¼-inch rulings, two pieces taped to yield 11 x 17 inches

white cotton or cotton/polyester blend, with medium body (a percale pillowcase works well), ½ yard or two 12 x 18-inch pieces

white or off-white quilting thread

quilting needle

sharp scissors (embroidery or dressmaking)

polyester fiberfill, approximately one ounce

sewing machine (optional)

knitting needle, crochet hook, or artists' paintbrush

Finished size: 15 inches tall

one square = 1"

Assembly

1. Enlarge the pattern given so it is 15 inches tall. One square on the grid equals one square inch (*see Drawing 61*).

2. Transfer the pattern of the angel outline onto a double thickness of fabric; the right sides of the fabric should face each other.

3. Machine or hand stitch directly on the outline of the angel, using small stitches. Be sure to stay on the marked line, and pay particular attention to the corners and curves. Leave a 3½-inch space open along one side of the skirt for turning.

4. Restitch over the initial stitching on curves under the arms and wings and at the neck.

5. With a pair of scissors, trim the material away to within ⅛ of an inch from the stitching, except at the open area along the skirt (leave a ½-inch seam there). Clip the seam allowance to the stitching at the corners under the arms and wings and at the neck as shown.

6. Turn the angel right side out. Use a crochet hook or the end of an artists' paintbrush to turn the small corners (hands, tip of hair, et cetera) completely.

7. Stuff the angel with polyester fiberfill. Stuffing should fill the angel but not be so thick you cannot stitch through it. The angel should be somewhat relaxed. Carefully distribute the filling uniformly and work it into the corners of the dress, hair, hands, sleeves, and wings. A knitting needle works well for this.

8. With an invisible stitch, close the stuffing hole along the skirt.

9. Using quilting thread, stitch the angel as shown in Drawing 62. Make small even stitches. You may wish to mark stitching lines with washable sewing chalk. Work with clean hands, and keep the angel in a plastic bag between quilting sittings.

10. Use an outline stitch and quilting thread to make the eyes and mouth.

11. Suspend the finished angel from the mantel or ceiling above the Christmas tree with white thread.

drawing 62

Photo by Alison Shaw

🌿 Angel cookie

Ingredients

1 cup soft butter
1 cup honey
6 to 7 cups all-purpose flour
2 teaspoons baking soda
1 teaspoon cinammon
¼ teaspoon nutmeg
½ teaspoon salt
½ cup cold strong tea
1 teaspoon vanilla

Cream the butter and honey. Sift all the dry ingredients together. Add them alternately with the liquid to the butter and honey, stirring after each addition. Cover the bowl of dough with wax paper and chill it overnight. In the morning, roll the dough to a ¼-inch thickness on a floured pastry board. Enlarge the pattern shown in Drawing 63 and transfer onto a piece of cardboard. Place the cardboard pattern on the dough and cut around the pattern with a sharp knife (an X-acto works well). Transfer the cut-out cookie to a cookie sheet.

Then, as you would mold clay, fashion strands of hair, buttons, and other accessories from the remains of the dough and decorate the angel with them. Paint the top of the cookie with beaten egg and bake for 10 minutes in a 350-degree oven.

These cookies, fresh, are very edible. But if you keep them and they grow hard, they also make attractive wall decorations.

drawing 63

one square = 1"

✿ Gilded cloth and paper angel

Make this angel ornament from cardboard, thread, cloth, doilies, and lace. Contrasting textures of hair, dress, and wing are accentuated when the finished angel is painted gold or silver.

Tools and materials

large kitchen knife
one Styrofoam ball, 1 inch in diameter
Liquitex acrylic gloss polymer medium
artists' paintbrush, No. 2 or No. 3
cardboard, 3 x 3 inches
heavy-duty white thread
scissors
two or three toothpicks
Elmer's Glue-All
Testor's Pla enamel, gold *or* silver
paper towels
pencil
lightweight cardboard, 6 x 6 inches (file folder, side of cereal box)
gold beading wire, No. 34, 8 inches
white lace seam binding (not the iron-on kind), about 10 inches, or white embroidery thread, one package
white thread
needle
paper lace doilies, 4 inches in diameter
wax paper

Finished size: 5¼ inches tall

Assembly

Head

1. With a sharp knife, cut the Styrofoam ball in half. You will be using only one of these pieces per angel. The rounded side is the front of the angel. Give the half you will be using two coats of acrylic gloss polymer medium, letting the medium dry between coats.

2. Cut strands of heavy-duty white thread for hair by winding thread around a 3 x 3-inch piece of cardboard 25 times. Cut through all thicknesses at each end of the cardboard to yield 50 strands of hair.

Photo by Edward E. Goodwin

71

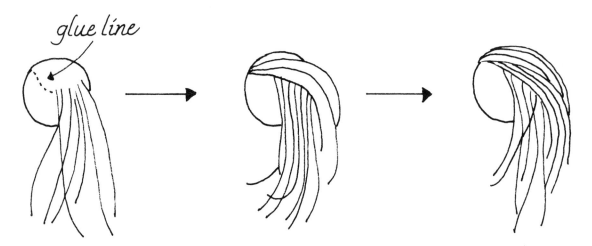

3. Insert a toothpick at an angle into the flat side of the Styrofoam ball to provide a handle while the hair is being applied.

4. Apply white glue to the rounded side (front) of the head, at the top, as in Drawing 64. Have a small pool of glue on a cardboard scrap nearby as well.

5. Begin applying the hair, one strand at a time, to the glued area of the head. Apply the lower area first, using about 10 strands (*see Drawing 64*). Be sure to imbed the end (root) of the strand into the glue. If needed, dip the strands first into the reservoir of glue. A toothpick often works better than fingers for imbedding the end of the strand into the glue on the head.

6. Apply the remaining strands, beginning at the forehead (*see the drawing*). These strands should eventually cover the root ends of the first group. Continue to apply hair until the arrangement is satisfactory and the scalp is covered. You may need to add a small drop of glue directly to empty places so that the strands will adhere.

7. Allow the hair to dry completely, preferably overnight.

8. Trim the hair to the desired length. Paint the head and hair silver or gold; both back and front should be painted. Blot the hair strands with a paper towel to absorb excess paint. Set the head aside.

Body

1. Cut the frame from the 6 x 6-inch piece of cardboard, using the pattern provided in Drawing 65. Punch a hole at the top of the frame with a toothpick and string the hole with an 8-inch length of gold wire. Twist the ends of the wire to form a loop for hanging.

drawing 64

drawing 65

cardboard frame pattern

2. Cut the material for the dress, using the dress pattern in Drawing 66. Avoid raveling the cut edges when you are handling the fabric.

3. Baste lace binding to the bottom of the dress and at the sleeve cuff, using small stitches and white thread. (If you prefer, you can decorate the dress with embroidery stitches instead of lace. Embroider the dress prior to cutting out the pattern. Use white single-strand embroidery floss. Effective stitches are the featherstitch and the French knot.)

4. Working on waxed paper, place the dress over the cardboard frame. With a paintbrush, wet the entire dress with acrylic gloss polymer medium. Create folds of the dress with your fingers, making sure the cardboard frame is not exposed, except at the hand and neck. Be sure as well that the hanging loop does not get covered with the medium or caught under the dress. When the medium dries it will stiffen the folds of the dress and "glue" the dress to the frame.

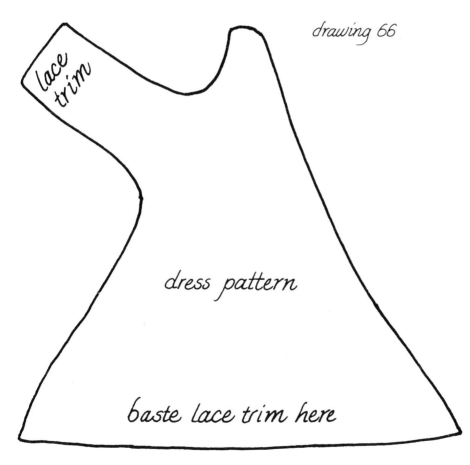

drawing 66

lace trim

dress pattern

baste lace trim here

5. Let the dress dry completely, preferably overnight. When it is dry, gently peel away the waxed paper.

6. Paint the dress and frame gold or silver, working the brush into the folds to cover all areas. Paint the back also.

7. When the paint is dry, attach the head to the frame tab with Elmer's glue.

Wing

1. Doilies come packaged stuck together. Do not separate one completely but leave two or three stuck together for stiffness.

2. Dab the edges of the doily in three or four places with a tiny drop of glue or polymer medium to make sure that individual doilies do not separate.

3. Paint the doily silver or gold, front and back; be sure the paint does not clog the openings in the doily design. Thin the paint and give the doily two coats if necessary to prevent clogging.

4. When the doily is completely dry, trim it to a circle approximately 2 inches in diameter, following the pattern on the doily.

5. Attach the wing to the angel at the shoulders with glue; the wing will overlap the frame in the back. See the finished angel in Drawing 67.

drawing 67

And the sound of the cherubims' wings was heard even to the outer court, as the voice of the almighty God when he speaketh.

Ezekiel 10:5

74

Photo by Peter Barry Chowka

❧ Copper angel candleholder

Tools and materials

soft sheet copper available from crafts-supply stores
cardboard
breadboard or plywood
solder
soldering flux
tin snips or heavy-duty shears
gloves
pliers
nail, scribe, or dull pencil
soldering gun or iron

Assembly

1. Trace the pattern pieces onto the cardboard (*see Drawings 68 and 69*).

2. Lay the copper on the breadboard or plywood and trace the pattern onto the metal.

3. Cut out the pieces. Double all pieces except the skirt, the candleholder, and the candle tray.

4. Using the nail, scribe, or dull pencil, press the designs into the appropriate pieces of metal. Draw on the hair, features, dress decoration, et cetera. Remember that you have both a back and a front to the candleholder, so score accordingly.

5. Bend the skirt piece into a cone.

6. Spread a little soldering flux along the seam of the skirt.

7. Heat the seam with the gun. When it is hot enough so that the solder, held close to the seam, will flow, hold the solder to the heated surface and move the gun along the surface (*see photo*). Remember that surfaces you solder get hot, so hold the metal pieces with your pliers while you work (or have an assistant hold them with the pliers). To cool soldered pieces quickly, dip them in cold water.

8. Solder the wings to the inside of the torso pieces.

9. Solder the torso pieces together in three or four places. Of course, the solder will be silver against the copper background, but the effect is not unattractive.

10. Spread the bottom of the torso pieces apart slightly and slip them into the top of the skirt (*see the photograph*). Solder.

11. Solder the sleeves together at the cuffs.

12. Spread the hands apart a little.

13. Solder the sleeves at the shoulders and elbows.

14. With the pliers, fold under the top of the candleholder piece. Then solder its ends together to make a circle. Solder the holder to the tray in which it will sit.

15. Put a candle in the holder to be sure that the sleeves are soldered in enough places to make them strong enough to bear the weight of the candle. If you need to strengthen the arms with more solder, do so.

Photos by Phyllis Méras

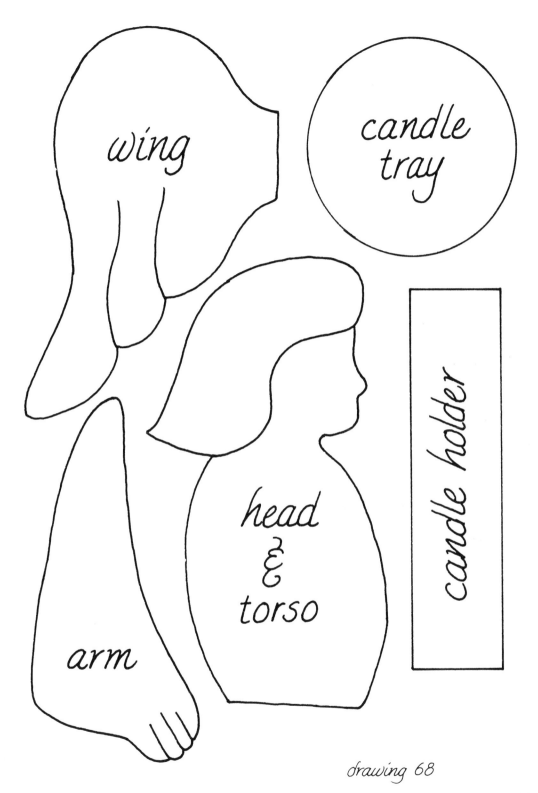

wing

candle tray

head & torso

arm

candle holder

drawing 68

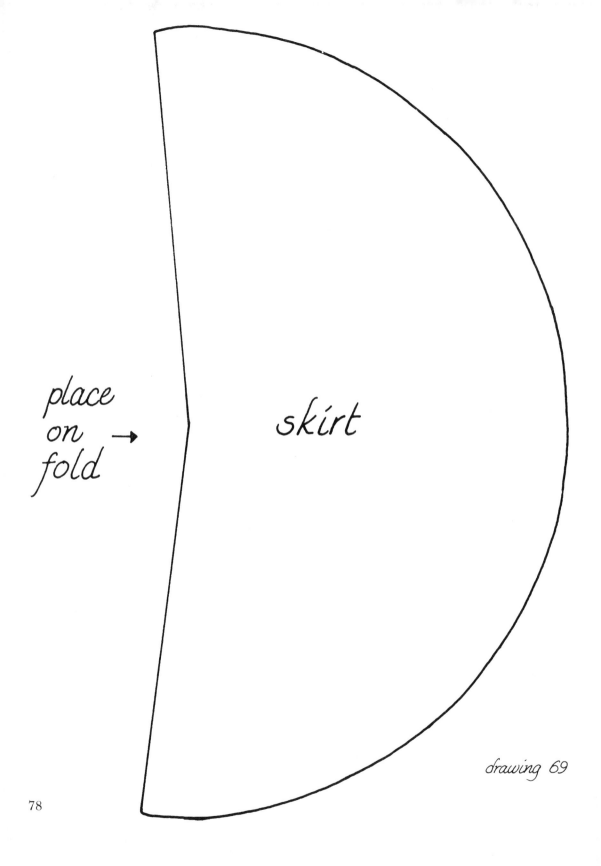

place
on →
fold

skirt

drawing 69

Swedish curled wood angels

Tools and materials

three toothpicks
three lengths of white embroidery floss, 4 feet long
hair spray
clear pine board, at least 14 inches long, 4 inches wide, and ½ an
    inch thick
vise
hand or power plane, set to $\frac{1}{64}$ of an inch
X-acto knife
paper clips, about six
small rubber bands
thread, any color
three balsa balls, ½ an inch in diameter
hand or power drill, with $\frac{3}{16}$-inch drill bit
Elmer's Glue-All
Liquitex acrylic colors, brown, blue, pink (or red and white)
artists' paintbrush, No. 00

Finished size: larger angel, 3½ inches tall; smaller, 2 inches tall

Assembly

1. Wind the three 4-foot lengths of single-strand white embroidery floss around the length of three tooth-picks. Spray each toothpick with hair spray and set aside for the curls to dry.

2. Cut wood strips with the plane as described in Feather Mobile Angel (pp. 34–35). Be sure to soak the wood first for at least eight hours. Depending upon the thickness of your board, you will probably be able to cut all but the wide strip for the large angel body from the edge of the board. Use the wide face of the board for the large angel body. Cut the individual pieces according to the sketches provided in Drawings 70 and 71, using an X-acto knife. Cut with the grain of the wood, going lengthwise of strips. Do this while the wood is still wet.

3. For the small angels, curl two sets of three body pieces and secure the narrow ends with a paper clip. Curl the skirt ends (the wider ends) slightly and hold them in place, curled, with string wound lengthwise around the

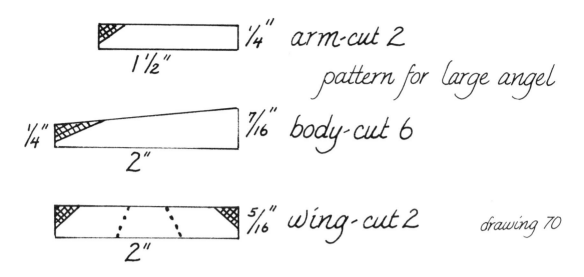

¼″ arm-cut 2

pattern for large angel

1½″

¼″ 7/16″ body-cut 6

2″

5/16″ *wing-cut 2*

2″

drawing 70

pieces. You should have two sets of small angel bodies, three pieces each. When these have dried, glue the three pieces together at the narrow ends of each body.

4. Shape two wings for the small angels, folding slightly at the dotted lines on the pattern guide. Hold this shape with a rubber band or string while the wood dries.

discard

shaded areas

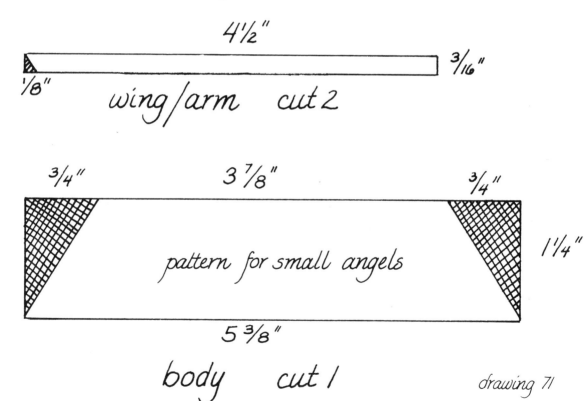

4½″

3/16″

⅛″ *wing/arm   cut 2*

¾″ 3 7/8″ ¾″

pattern for small angels

1¼″

5 3/8″

body   cut 1

drawing 71

5. Each small angel has one arm piece. Position both arm pieces side by side, having beveled ends touching. Curl each unbeveled end slightly toward the center, for hands. Secure each hand with thread or a rubber band while the wood dries.

6. For the large angel, curl the body piece as shown in the photograph; clip with a paper clip while the wood dries. The fold at the top should be pointed so it will fit into the head later.

7. For the large angel's wings, fold each of the two wing strips in half crosswise and lap the ends over one another. The ends should cross and extend about ¾ inch. One extension from each wing is the arm; the other extension secures the wing to the angel's back. Use a paper clip at each junction to hold the wing as it dries.

8. While the wood strips are drying, prepare the heads. Clamp the balsa balls in the vise, one at a time, and drill a ³⁄₁₆-inch hole, ¼ of an inch deep. Be sure to protect the balsa wood balls in the vise with a layer of cardboard or other scrap wood.

9. Glue the narrow end of each small angel body into the hole in a balsa ball. You may need to trim the body so it will fit the hole. Attach the large angel body to the third ball in the same way with a dab of Elmer's glue. Be sure to let the glue dry completely before you continue.

10. When the hair spray on the embroidery thread has dried, gently unwind the thread from the toothpick, retaining the curls. Apply Elmer's glue to the crown area of each balsa ball, and glue the curls to the heads. Distribute the hair evenly over the crown area, pressing the curls so there are no large loops not secured.

11. Glue a wing section to each of the small angels, attaching it to the angel's back.

12. While the glue is drying on the small angels' wings, affix the two crossed wings to the large angel (*see Drawing 72*). The arms, which are the wing extensions, should be visible from the front of the angel.

13. Position and secure the arms to the small angels, overlapping each of the inner arms (beveled end) to join the angels. Refer to the photograph.

14. With the tiny paintbrush, give each angel a face with acrylic color.

15. Thread a needle with a 9-inch length of white embroidery floss and catch a few of the curls at the back of the large angel's head. Knot the thread for a hanging loop. Attach a loop to the head of one small angel.

drawing 72

Photo by Alison Shaw

❧ Angel in an egg

Tools and materials

egg
crewel needle or skewer
cuticle scissors or hand-held Dremel motor tool
cotton
Glitter Glue
Diamond Dust
Elmer's Glue-All
miniature angel figure from a crafts-supply store
acrylic paints
gold braid
gold cord
bell cap from a jewelry-findings shop
decoupage satin finish or Regal Egg Sheen
toothpick
ribbon
beading

Assembly

1. Draw an oval on the side of the egg.

2. Poke a small hole in each end of the egg with a crewel needle or skewer and gently blow out the egg. Cut out the oval portion marked on the shell. If you don't want to blow out the egg, simply begin immediately cutting a small hole in the center of the oval with the cuticle scissors; then, going round and round, enlarge the hole until you have cut out the whole oval that you marked. This is the messier way of removing the egg, but it keeps the interior of the shell moist, which is desirable to prevent cracking. If you have a Dremel hand motor tool, it may be used for the cutting.

3. If you like, paint the egg inside and out with acrylics. Or you may prefer the natural egg color.

4. Spread Elmer's glue on the bottom of a piece of cotton and insert it into the bottom of the egg.

5. Spray the cotton with Glitter Glue and sprinkle Diamond Dust on it.

6. Glue the angel, an artificial tree, or whatever else you like into the cotton.

7. Spread glue around the edge of the oval and attach the gold braid.

8. To hang the egg from the Christmas tree, put a dab of glue on the top and attach a bell cap and a piece of gold cord.

Photo by Alison Shaw

83

❧ Wooden angel

Tools and materials

block of holly, ⅝ of an inch thick
cardboard
band saw or coping saw
pocket knife
wood rasp
rat-tail file
120C and 220A sandpaper
Delft clear finish

Assembly

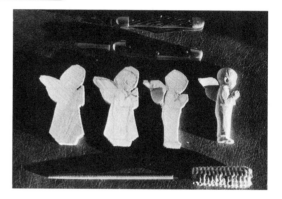

Four steps in carving an angel. (Photos by Phyllis Méras)

1. Draw an angel on a piece of cardboard. Cut it out and trace it onto the holly wood. (Holly wood is best because the wood stays white, according to Ruth Hawkins of Warne, North Carolina, who has been making little angels for more than 30 years.)

2. Saw the figure from the wood with a band saw or coping saw.

3. Fashion the features of the angel with the knife and wood rasp. Use the square point of the knife to cut lines and the sharp point for general feature carving, rounding out wings, et cetera. When you are carving the angel's face, be sure to take only the smallest of chips out. Go cautiously, for you can easily destroy a face.

4. After carving, use the wood rasp and rat-tail file to remove carving marks.

5. When the carving suits you, sand the angel, first with the 120C paper, then with the 220A.

6. Coat with Delft clear finish to keep the wood clean.

Photo by Alison Shaw

❧ Straw angel

Tools and materials

eight 3-inch straws for the wings
ten 6-inch straws for the dress
a needle
red crochet cotton
a pipe cleaner
Elmer's Glue-All
a craft bead head from a crafts-supply shop
gold thread

Assembly

1. Pick the straw for the angel at harvest time in late summer or early fall, preferably before there is much rain, for it will turn straw brown.

2. Soak the straw for four hours in warm water.

3. Clean the straw by cutting away the outer joints and removing the outer casing. From each straw, you should get three straws of different lengths.

4. Mark each of the wing straws in the center with a pencil. Push a fine needle through them at the pencil mark.

5. Wind crochet cotton around the straws twice close under the needle and pull the thread tight. The straws will expand into a flat double fan. Tie a firm double knot. Snip the thread, leaving ¼ of an inch. Remove the needle.

6. Take the ten dress straws and gather them into a bunch 3 inches in diameter. Tie them tightly in the middle with red thread and they will flare slightly.

7. Straw by straw, bend the upper section of these dress straws down over the lower section (*as in Drawing 73*), turning the bundle as you work, thus covering all the thread. If you hold all these straws tightly together there will be a resultant hole in the middle of the bundle.

8. Cut off a pipe cleaner to about 2 inches in length. Dip its end into Elmer's glue and insert it into the craft bead, creating a head and neck. Insert this head and neck into the hole in the center of the straws.

9. Now lift up one of the straws at the back of the head and place the wings under that straw. Draw the straw back into place and tie the bodice ½ inch below the neck with the red thread. Tie it very tightly so the skirt flares as much as possible.

10. Use the lowest of the wing straws for the arms. Bend them forward to make elbows and tie the wrists close together near the body with the red thread. Turn the ends to make tiny hands clasped in prayer.

11. Tie fine gold thread around the angel's neck to hang it from the tree.

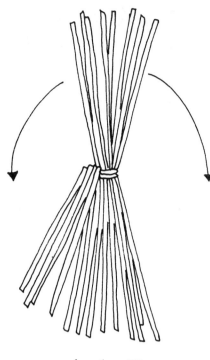

drawing 73

❧ Macramé angel

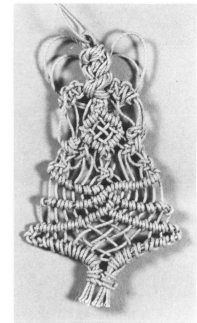

Materials

pink macramé cord cut to:
- two 20-inch cords for the body
- four 8-inch cords for the arms
- two 16-inch cords for the diamond
- one 8-inch cord for the hanging loop
- one 8-inch cord for the wings
- one 6-inch cord for the wings

Elmer's glue

Finished size: 4 inches tall

Assembly

1. Take the two 20-inch cords and double them, with the fold at the top.

2. Make two overhand knots, one on top of the other, ½ an inch down from the fold/loop at the top (*see Drawing 74*). These knots are the head.

3. Take the four 8-inch cords and, using a half knot, tie them below the two overhand knots (head) to form the neck (*see Drawing 75*).

4. Next, take the 8-inch cords and make an arm, using two successive square knots and then an overhand knot. Do the same with the other arm (*see Drawing 76*).

5. Go back to where the arms were joined to the trunk and, picking up the four cords, tie a square knot below the neck (*see Drawing 76*).

Photo by Edward E. Goodwin

drawing 74

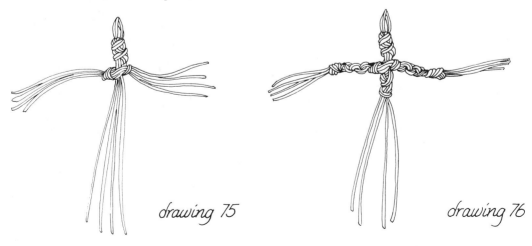

drawing 75

drawing 76

87

6. Attach the two 16-inch cords, doubled, through the back of the knot you have just made. Tie in the cords the same way that sales tags are looped. You will now have eight cords to make the diamond (*see Drawing 77*).

7. To make the diamond at the angel's chest, tie three double half hitches on the four right-hand cords (*see Drawing 78*). Do the same on the four left-hand cords (*see Drawing 79*). Weave these eight cords together and finish the bottom half of the diamond by reversing the half hitches (*see Drawing 80*).

8. The four cords from the right arm and the two uppermost cords of the diamond are joined in an over-hand knot, forming the right hand. Do the same for the left hand (*as in Drawing 81*).

9. With the next two cords of the diamond, right-hand side, make a square knot. This will be next to the right hand. Do the same for the left side.

10. You should now have 16 cords to work with. Take the first four cords on the right side and make a square knot. Do the same on the left side.

drawing 77

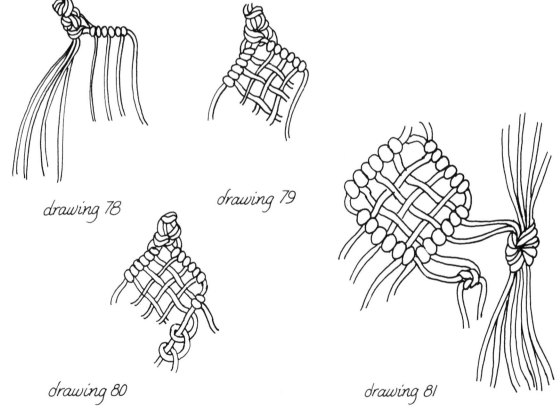

drawing 78

drawing 79

drawing 80

drawing 81

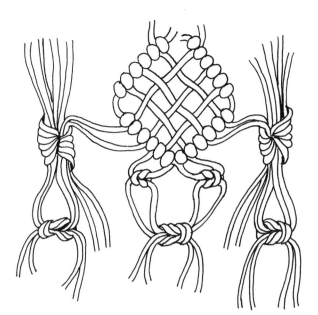

drawing 82

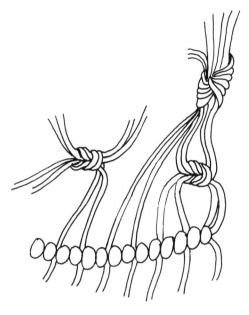

drawing 83

wings

drawing 84

11. Next, pick up the center four cords and make a square knot (*see Drawing 82*).

12. Divide the cords (eight on each side); beginning in the middle, work half hitches toward the sides to form the first tier (*Drawing 83*). Begin in the middle and work outward to make the second and third tiers the same way.

13. Weave the center eight cords.

14. Make half hitches to form the bottom tier of the skirt, working inward to enclose the woven section.

15. For feet, divide the cords. With one cord from the right side, tie three half hitches, one under the other, around other cords. Do the same for the left foot.

16. Insert an 8-inch cord through the uppermost loop (top of the head). Knot this loop near the ends to make a hanging loop for the angel.

17. Take the 6- and 8-inch cords and loop them together, to form wings, as shown in Drawing 84. Glue the wings to the back of the angel at the knot above the diamond.

A woodland angel may be made (left) of a fir or spruce cone, trumpet vine bean pod wings, and an acorn head; or (right) of a pine cone, maple seed pod wings, and a bean head. (Photos by Peter Barry Chowka)

🌿 Woodland angel

Tools and materials

Douglas fir or Colorado blue spruce cone
an acorn
trumpet vine bean pods or milkweed pods, gathered in the fall
jute rope, 6-strand
spray starch
Elmer's Glue-All
cornhusk
acrylic paints
florists' wire, No. 26
scissors
small hand drill
two small index cards
thread

Finished size: 3 to 4 inches

Assembly

1. With the hand drill and a small bit, drill a hole from the top to the bottom of the acorn. (If it is fresh, you may be able to run a darning needle through it.) Insert one

end of the florists' wire, which has been dipped in glue. Wind the other end around the petals at the bottom of the cone.

2. Soak the trumpet vine or milkweed pods in water overnight.

3. In the morning, cut the pods so that the lower part of the pod makes the wing; a sliver of the upper part, the arm. Set aside.

4. Cut two pieces of 6-strand jute rope, one the length you would like the angel's hair to be; the other, the length for bangs. Stitch the hair to the index cards across the center of the strands and comb it out. If it is too frazzly, spray it with spray starch.

5. Apply Elmer's glue to the top of the acorn. Remove the hair and bangs from the cards and glue them on the acorn head. Tie a strip of cloth around the head and neck while the hair dries to keep it in place.

6. Touch the ends of the pods with glue where they will be attached to the cone.

7. Glue these pod arms and wings onto the cone a petal or two below the head. The arms go underneath the wings.

8. Soak a cornhusk in warm water about 10 minutes. From the husk cut a ¾-inch square to make a scroll. Make the scroll by rolling the piece of wet husk around a pencil, then letting it dry.

9. Touch up the edges of the cone, the face, et cetera, with acrylic paints.

Photo by Edward E. Goodwin

Yarn angel

Tools and materials

white crewel or baby yarn, approximately 10 yards
scissors
two pieces of cardboard, each 4 x 4 inches (from file folder or
    index card)
5 inches of gold cording, about 1/16 of an inch thick
white thread
embroidery thread for hair (brown, yellow, et cetera),
    approximately 2 yards
embroidery thread for face (black, pink)
embroidery needle
artists' paintbrush, No. 3
Testors Pla enamel paint, gold

Finished size: 4 inches tall

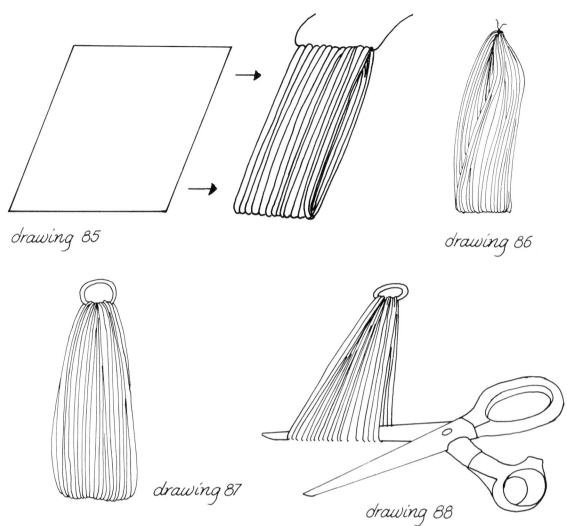

drawing 85

drawing 86

drawing 87

drawing 88

Assembly

1. Cut off a length of yarn one yard long and re-serve it for tying.

2. Wind the remaining yarn around one of the pieces of cardboard 40 times.

3. Carefully slide the yarn off the cardboard, retaining the loops (*see Drawing 85*).

4. Tie the strands at one end of the loops with some of the reserved yarn. Knot and clip close to the knot (*see Drawing 86*).

5. Tie the gold cord loosely around the strands over the tied area, leaving ¼-inch clearance from yarn. Slide the knot underneath (*see Drawing 87*).

6. Cut the bottom loops of yarn. They should be even (*see Drawing 88*).

7. With some of the reserved yarn, tie off the head ⅞ of an inch below the top of the yarn. Wind two or three times and tie the knot in the back. Clip the yarn close to the knot (*see Drawing 89*).

drawing 89

8. Lay the angel face up on the working surface. To make the arms, pull 15 strands of yarn from each side below the neckline, as in left side of Drawing 90.

9. With tying yarn, wrap and tie the arms 1 inch from the body; leave the knots in the front. This forms the wrists. Trim the arm strands to ¼ of an inch below the wrists (*see right arm in Drawing 90*).

10. Tie off the waist 1 inch below the neckline with tying yarn (*see Drawing 91*).

11. Fold the arms across the waist so the hands touch and secure them invisibly to the body with the needle and white thread (*see Drawing 92*).

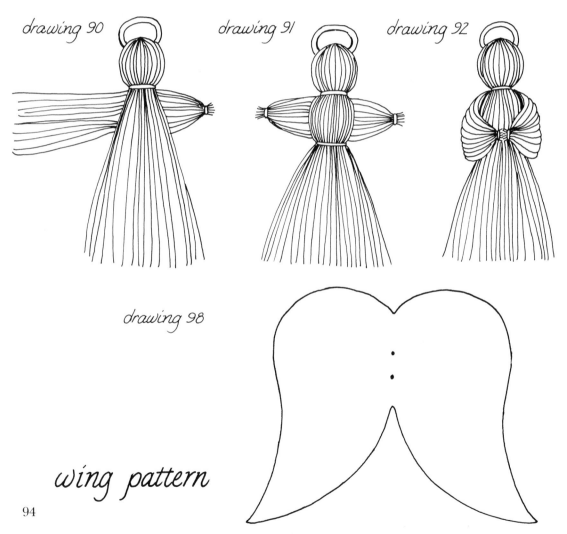

drawing 90

drawing 91

drawing 92

drawing 98

wing pattern

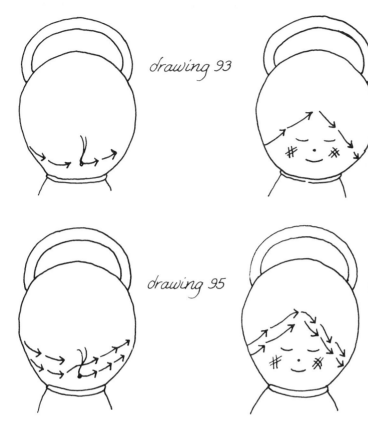

drawing 93

drawing 94

drawing 95

drawing 96

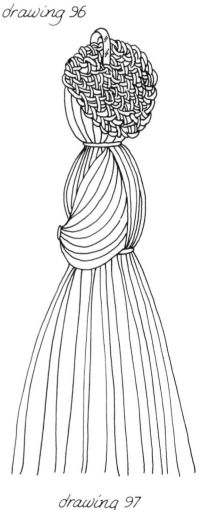

12. For the hair, braid three 24-inch lengths of 6-strand embroidery floss and knot each end. Attach the braid to the head, beginning at the nape of the neck and working in a circular pattern toward the front and across the forehead (*see Drawings 93–97*). Secure the braid to the head with a single strand of matching embroidery floss.

13. Embroider the face with a single strand of embroidery floss: black for eyes and nose and pink for the mouth. Use a tiny amount of lipstick or rouge for the cheeks, applying it with a Q-tip or your fingertip.

14. From the remaining 4 x 4-inch piece of cardboard, cut the wings from the pattern provided in Drawing 98. Using an artists' paintbrush (No. 3), paint both sides of the wings gold. Let the wings dry completely. With a needle, punch holes in the wings as indicated on the pattern. Attach the wings to the angel's back with white thread. Carefully touch up the white thread against the wings with gold paint.

15. Attach a hanging loop to the head behind the halo, using white thread or embroidery floss.

16. Trim the skirt to a uniform length if necessary.

drawing 97

This pretty angel was stamped from brass. (Photo by Edward E. Goodwin)

But ye are come unto mount Sion, and unto the city of the living God, the heavenly Jerusalem, and to an innumerable company of angels.

Hebrews 12:22

Angel sandcasting

Tools and materials

cardboard gift box
damp sand
plaster of Paris
small solid figure of an angel (may be pottery or glass)

Assembly

1. To make a sandcasting of an angel to set on the mantel at Christmastime, fill a cardboard gift box with damp sand. Press a solid figure of an angel into it. The figure should not be so thick that, pressed, it goes all the way to the bottom of the sand.

2. Remove the figure and gently pour in the plaster of Paris mixed according to the directions on the package. Both mix and pour slowly to make sure no bubbles form. When you pour, the consistency should be that of light cream.

3. When you are sure the plaque is dry, tear away the cardboard and your angel is ready to display.

4. If you want a little color around your figure, half bury a few pieces of colored glass in the sand around the figure before you pour in the plaster of Paris. Just be sure not to bury them too deep in the sand or they will not be transferred to the sandcasting.

Photos by Alison Shaw

Photo by Phyllis Méras

Tissue paper angels

Materials

a package of tissue paper for gift wrapping, colored or white
two pounds of paraffin
white thread

Assembly

1. From one piece of the tissue paper, cut as many 9 x 13½-inch rectangles as you wish to have angels.

2. From a second piece, make the wings, tracing the pattern in Drawing 99 along a fold of the paper so that when the pattern is cut, the two wings will be attached at the base.

3. Holding each 9 x 13½-inch rectangle the long way, gather the sides in toward you as if you were making a yarn doll. Then fold over the middle to make a head and tie it with thread, but don't cut off the thread. You will use it later to dip the angel in the paraffin.

4. Lift the sides of the tissue rectangle and insert the wing pieces under the neck, pulling the wings out a bit from the body.

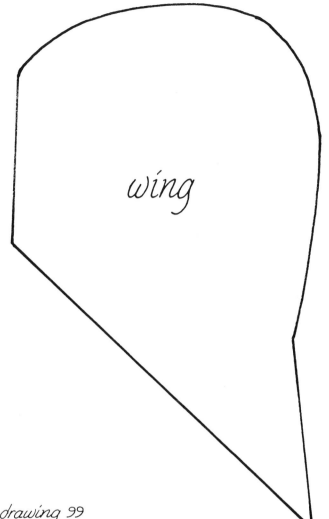

wing

drawing 99

5. With another piece of thread, form a waist, thereby also holding the wings in place. Again, don't cut off the thread.

6. Heat the paraffin in an old pot, bringing the wax just to the melting point.

7. Dip each angel head first into it, covering the wings and the head with wax. Then, immediately, turn the angel right side up and dip the skirt in the paraffin. Hang the angel right side up to dry. These angels can be either hung from driftwood as a mobile or simply dangled from the Christmas tree.

Photo by Alison Shaw

Golden Spackle angel

Tools and materials

a wire coat hanger that is fairly flexible
a Styrofoam egg
Spackle
old sheeting, preferably cotton
old cotton mop
wide masking tape
paper handkerchiefs
Elmer's Glue-All
paper towels
a sheet of cardboard or poster board

100

spray paint, gold
a thin mail order catalogue, preferably one fastened together
    with staples
wire snips
sturdy scissors for cutting cardboard
old tray or cookie sheet to work on
pliers
wax paper
old kettle for mixing Spackle

Finished size: 18 inches

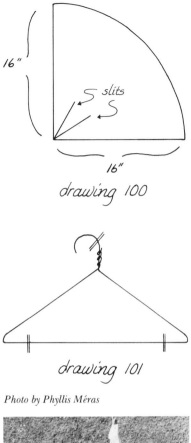

drawing 100

Assembly

1. On the cardboard or poster board, draw a quarter of a circle that has 16-inch sides. This will become the angel's body.

2. At the point of this quarter circle, cut two slits 3 inches deep, pointing directly toward the bottom of the quarter circle (*see Drawing 100*). These should divide the point into thirds. Be sure that the slits are cut straight down, not at an angle. Into these, you will eventually insert the angel's arms.

3. Roll the cardboard quarter circle into a cone shape. Do this gently so there are no creases in the cardboard.

4. With the masking tape, tape the edges of the cone together around its circumference, not up and down. When you are through, you should have a cone 6 inches across at the base. Be sure that you have rolled the cone tightly and taped it securely. When the cone is finished, set it down to be sure that it stands straight. If it does not, trim it across the bottom.

5. Now straighten the hook of the coat hanger with the pliers, but do not untwist it. Cut off the top about 1½ inches above the twist. Cut a piece out of the base of the hanger, leaving about 2 inches on either side below where the hanger bends (*see Drawing 101*). Discard the cut-out piece. What remains will become the arms and the neck of the angel.

6. Insert the wire armature into the slits in the peak of the cone. Fasten it in place with the masking tape. You should now have a neck protruding from the top of the cone and arms from each side. Bend the armature to make shoulders and elbows, and into whatever position you wish the arms to have (*see the photo*). Remember that the elbows should bend about where you wish the angel's waist to be.

drawing 101

Photo by Phyllis Méras

7. Poke the Styrofoam head onto the wire neck. If you have not been able to find a Styrofoam egg shape, you can sand a Styrofoam ball into an egg shape by laying it on a table and sanding it to the shape you want with rough sandpaper. If you would like features on the face of your angel, with your thumb gently make indentations for the eyes, et cetera.

8. Mix a small quantity of Spackle with water, following the directions on the package. Add enough water to make the mixture the consistency of cream.

9. Tear up a little of the paper toweling into ½-inch strips. Dip them into the Spackle. Smooth them onto the Styrofoam face.

10. Dip a piece of sheeting 10 inches wide and ¾ of an inch wide into the Spackle. Smooth off the excess and, starting on the top of the head, crisscross the material in back of the head, again in front of the neck, then around under the armpits, and, if there is any extra, wind it loosely around the upper arm.

11. Crumple more paper toweling, but do not dip it in Spackle. Use this to give shape to the angel's bust.

12. Cut a piece of sheeting 14 x 1½ inches and dip this into the Spackle (mix more if you need to). Smooth off the excess and bind the crumpled paper towel to the front of the angel with it. Start in front. Wind the strip around to the back; crisscross over the shoulders; go around the neck and under the arms — in whatever pattern you choose that will secure the bust to the cone and the arms and neck.

13. With the pliers, form loop-like hands at the ends of the arms (see Drawing 102). Take two 7 x ½-inch strips of cloth and dip them, one at a time, into the Spackle. Smooth off the excess and, one at a time, fashion the hands, starting at the inside of each loop, crisscrossing around the wrist. Cover the wire and fill in the hole, but be sure not to make a club-like hand. Any extra material may be wound up the forearm till it reaches the bust on the upper arm. This will help to give shape to the arms and shoulders.

14. By this time, you may need to mix up more Spackle again. Take the two 14½ x 7½-inch arm strips. Dip one into the Spackle and smooth off the excess. Turn the long sides of the strips under about 1 inch so it looks as if they were hemmed. Starting at one wrist, loop the sleeve piece loosely around the arm and then up to the shoulder. The effect you want is of a draped sleeve (see the photo-

Photo by Phyllis Méras

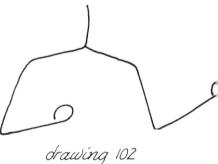

drawing 102

graph). End under the arm at the shoulder. Be sure the ends are camouflaged.

15. Repeat for the second sleeve.

16. Cut a piece of sheeting 38 x 11 inches and make a 4½-inch slit in it at the center of the top; this will be used to make the robe. Dip it into the Spackle (it will probably use up nearly a full pot) and smooth off the excess. Put the robe over the angel's head and drape it toga-fashion, with thick and bulky folds, turning it under at the bottom to make a hem. Bring the material together at the sides so no cone shows underneath. Use your imagination in doing the draping. Arrange the material so that the heavy folds are at the bottom and so that the robe sweeps toward the back in a train-like effect.

17. Tie an 8-inch-long string around the center of the wings and then firmly around the neck.

18. Dip an 8 x 2-inch piece, which will be used for the neckpiece, into the Spackle. Fold in the long edges in a hem-like way. Drape the neck piece across the front of the throat to cover the strings. You can wedge any extra ends of neck piece under the wings to help them stand out more from the body.

19. Dip some of the mop strings, cut to whatever length you wish the hair to be, into the Spackle. Smooth off the excess and lay the strings across the head to resemble hair. Remember that most hairdos have a part.

20. Place the angel upright on more cardboard. Trace around its skirt and cut out a base. If you would like the angel to be solidly set, tape a small stone to the center of the piece of cardboard that is to make the base. Then slather glue around the edge of the top of the cardboard base. Put the angel on it and set it all up to dry. Depending upon the weather conditions, this could take several days.

21. Cut a tiny book from the catalogue (around one of its staples) and glue it into the angel's hands. A pin will hold it in place until it dries.

22. Spray the figure with gold spray paint.

Photo by Phyllis Méras

Photos by Phyllis Méras

Wax angels
for candlesticks

Tools and materials

paraffin
double boiler or coffee can inside an old pot
angel-shaped cookie cutters
cookie sheet (sprayed with Pam)
egg beater
candles
iridescent glitter or gold Rub 'n' Buff and acrylic paints

Assembly

Photo by Edward E. Goodwin

1. Melt a block of paraffin in the double boiler.

2. Pour it to a depth of a little less than ¼ of an inch in a cookie sheet sprayed with Pam.

3. Cool the paraffin to room temperature. Then use the cookie cutter to cut angel shapes in it.

4. Heat the bottom of the cookie sheet slightly with a warm cloth or an iron and carefully remove the angels with a spatula.

5. Take some of the remaining melted wax and beat it to whipped cream consistency.

6. Apply a blob of the whipped wax to the backs of the wax cutouts and affix them, while the wax is still soft and creamy, to a candle laid flat on a table. If you like, you can form clouds with a little extra whipped wax and attach them, too.

7. Before the angels are completely dry, they may be sprinkled with iridescent glitter.

8. These angels can also be decorated with acrylic paints and the edges antiqued with gold Rub 'n' Buff.

(If you have angel-shaped cookie molds instead of cookie cutters, the wax can be poured into them, to set. Be sure to spray the molds with Pam.)

❧ Clothespin angel

Materials

one old-fashioned knob clothespin (available in crafts-supply stores)
one ¾-inch wooden bead-craft head
white cloth-covered florists' wire
5 inches of 4-inch-wide, gathered, single-edged lace
21 inches of 1-inch-wide lace
white thread
one gold jump ring, ½ to ¾ of an inch in diameter, or gold sequin trim
Elmer's Glue-All

Assembly

1. Make a seam in the 5-inch piece of lace and gather it to fit just over the knob on the top of the clothespin. A bit of glue will help to hold it in place.

2. Make a 4-part bow of the more delicate 21-inch lace. Sew it in the middle and gather it so that it will stick out like wings. Sew it just under the gathered top of the back of the angel, about ¼ of an inch from the top.

3. Make a waist for the angel's dress by winding thread tightly just under the knob. Adjust the skirt so the fullness is in front.

4. Glue on the bead head. If you cannot find one with the face already painted on, paint one with acrylics.

5. Glue a halo of gold sequin trim onto the head or use the jump ring, glued on.

6. Cut the white florists' wire to make the arms. Sew them securely (hiding the stitches) under the wings. Make loop-like hands, if you like, from the ends of the wire.

October is the month of the angels.

Photo by Phyllis Méras

Ribbon angel

Materials

ribbon, 6 to 8 inches long
one pipe cleaner
one bell cap from a jewelry-findings or crafts-supply store
one wooden bead with a painted face (available in most crafts
        stores)
embroidery floss
Elmer's Glue-All

Assembly

1. Tie the ribbon into a bow and set it aside.
2. Double over the pipe cleaner and dip the ends into Elmer's glue. Insert them into the hole in the bead. Let it dry.
3. Cut the floss to make hair. Glue it in place.
4. Glue on the bell cap to make a halo.
5. Insert the pipe cleaner with its head into the knot of the bow.

Photo by Alison Shaw

❧ Angel ornaments

Materials

picture wire, about 2 inches for each angel
Styrofoam ball
Decal-it
pictures of angels from Christmas cards, napkins, wrapping
    paper, et cetera
gesso
satin-finish decoupage medium
Elmer's Glue-All
fine glass eggery beads from a crafts-supply store
a little nylon net and a soft cloth

Finished size: about 3 inches in diameter

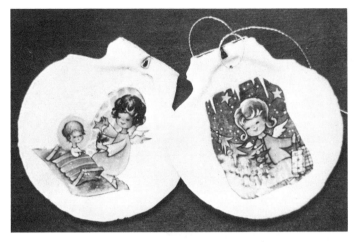

Scallop shells, decorated with Christmas card designs (upper left), make pretty tree dangles. Spray them with Krylon after the pictures have been transferred. (Photo by Phyllis Méras)

This cheery angel (upper right) from a Christmas card was transferred with Decal-it to a piece of thin plywood, from a crafts shop, that has been cut with a hacksaw to the angel's shape. After the transfer was made, the angel was sprayed with Krylon. (Photo by Phyllis Méras)

A smooth stone or a cake of soap can also become the base for an angel removed from a card with Decal-it (center). If you use soap, paint it with a thin coat of wax after you have transferred the picture. (Photo by Phyllis Méras)

Assembly

1. Apply a little glue to the ends of a twisted loop of wire and insert it as a hanger into the top of the Styrofoam ball.

2. Paint the ball with two coats of gesso. Dry.

3. Lift the prints you have selected from their magazines, cards, et cetera, as directed on the Decal-it package.

4. Glue them to the ball with Decal-it, overlapping their edges so no part of the ball shows through.

5. Let the ball dry.

6. Coat it with satin-finish decoupage medium or with Elmer's glue.

7. While the ball is still wet, sprinkle on some fine glass eggery beads, or, if you prefer a soft finish, when the decoupage medium or glue has dried, evenly brush on a thin coat of paraffin. Rub it smooth with nylon net. Then buff it with a soft cloth.

109

🍂 Leaf angel

Materials

two sumac leaves for arms
two large oak or maple leaves for the body
half of a walnut shell for the head
dried grass for a halo
dried straw flowers for a bouquet
silicone glue
Krylon No. 1311 matte-finish spray

Assembly

1. Glue the maple or oak leaves on top of each other, using the broad base of the leaves at the top to make the shoulders.

Photo by Phyllis Méras

2. Glue on the sumac arms.

3. Glue on the snippets of grass that will make the halo.

4. Apply glue to the straw flowers and fold the arms over them so they are held in place.

5. Spray with Krylon finish.

Photo by Peter Barry Chowka

❧ Angel puzzle

Tools and materials

Any good calendar picture of an angel. Don't use one that is
 printed on shiny paper, because it will not cut well. A large
 museum Christmas card will do, but 5 x 8 inches is the
 minimum size that can be used.
³⁄₁₆-inch bass plywood, available from woodcraft-supply stores
a jigsaw with a fine saw-tooth blade
Elmer's Glue-All
rolling pin
spatula
fine sandpaper, No. 100 or 125

Assembly

 1. Spread the glue evenly and not too thickly over
the wood with a spatula.

2. Lay the picture (right side up) on the plywood. Press it gently with a rolling pin until there are no more bubbles. Let the picture dry.

3. Mark the picture off across the top into segments ¾ to 1 inch wide. Use a light pencil. Then start cutting from top to bottom, making reverse French curves. Remember that you will need locks — either nubs or voids — on at least two sides of every piece.

4. Once you have cut the first strip longitudinally, remove the remainder of the puzzle from the saw table and cut the first strip horizontally. Reassemble the strip on your worktable.

5. Cut the second strip in the same manner and reassemble it next to the first. Proceed in this manner until the whole puzzle is cut and assembled. Depending on the size of your picture, you should have between 180 and 270 pieces.

6. Turn the entire puzzle over and sand the bottom lightly.

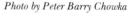
Photo by Peter Barry Chowka

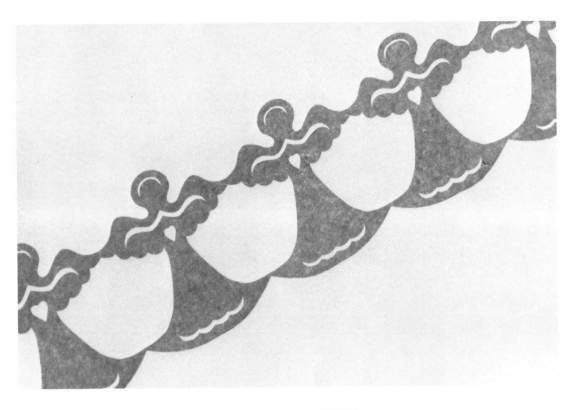

🎄 Paper-doll angels

Photos by Edward E. Goodwin

The familiar paper-doll technique is used at Christmastime to produce strings of paper angels. These are wonderful tree decorations. You can also cut them from tissue paper and paste them to boxes and wrapped packages, as shown in the photograph. Colored tissue paper on a white background is recommended. (White paper loses its color when glued to a darker background.)

Tools and materials

paper, white or colored, one 8½ x 14-inch (legal-sized) piece
sharp scissors
pencil
Scotch tape
Liquitex acrylic gloss polymer medium (if using tissue paper)
artists' paintbrush, medium size, about a No. 4 (if using tissue paper)

Finished size: 3½ inches tall

Assembly for four angels in a row

1. Design an angel 3½ inches high and about 1¾ inches wide, or use one of the designs provided in the photograph or in Drawing 103. When making your sketch, remember that no cutting lines can go through the angel completely either horizontally or vertically.

2. Fold the 8½ x 14-inch piece of paper in half to make a piece measuring 8½ x 7 inches. Make a sharp fold and be sure the corners are even.

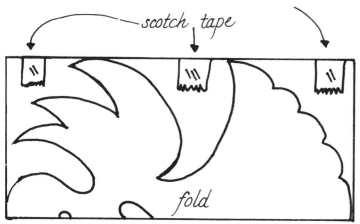

scotch tape

cut on solid lines

do not cut on fold

fold

drawing 103

3. Fold the paper again to make an 8½ x 3¼-inch piece, making a sharp fold.

4. Fold the paper a third time to yield a piece 8½ inches by a little more than 1¾ inches.

5. Cut this strip in half crosswise. You should now have two folded pieces of paper, 4¼ inches tall by about 1¾ inches wide, from which you can make two strings of angels.

6. Trace your design lightly onto paper. It is better to make only a few rough guidelines if you can.

7. If your design is complex, tape the edges that will be discarded with short pieces of Scotch tape (the Scotch tape should not extend onto the design — *see Drawing 103*).

8. Cut out the design, using smooth cuts. Cut the inner parts first.

If you are using tissue paper, you can fold the paper more times and still be able to get a good design (and more angels!). If you wish to apply the angels to a surface, lay the angels down and paint over them, with acrylic gloss polymer medium. Brush in one direction and work from the center out toward the edge of the design.

114

Photo by Edward E. Goodwin

🎄 Potato print angels

Design and print your own wrapping paper and greeting cards with a potato, a knife, and an ink pad. Ink pads are available in Christmas colors (red, green, violet, blue). Try cutting two identical designs and alternating the colors.

Tools and materials

a large baking potato
a large sharp kitchen knife
a small sharp paring knife or a penknife with a long point
white paper, glazed shelf paper, or tissue paper
construction paper or unruled 5 x 8-inch index cards, for
      greeting cards
Sanford's inked stamp pad, 3 x 4½ inches, red, violet, green, or
     blue
paper towels

Finished size: 2¾ inches high

Assembly

1. On a piece of paper, sketch the design you wish to use. Keep your first angel simple; straight lines are easier to work with than curved areas. The design should be no larger than 2¼ x 3½ inches so it will fit in the stamp pad box. Shade in the area you wish to be imprinted. Everything else will have to be cut away when you transfer the angel to the potato.

2. Wash and dry the potato. With one clean stroke cut the potato in half lengthwise to get the largest surface area for carving.

3. Using your sketch as a guide, outline your design onto the potato, using a sharp-pointed knife. Make the cuts at least ¼ of an inch deep.

4. Working from the edge of the potato about ¼ of an inch down from the cut surface, cut away the potato from the design. You may need to make small inroads to the design. Remember not to cut into your design.

5. When you have cut away all the potato from the design, to a depth of ¼ or ⅜ of an inch below the surface, view the potato from the side. Make sure the design stands out above all other parts of the potato.

6. Blot the potato gently on a paper towel. Begin printing right away or the potato will become mushy and green.

7. Gently press the potato onto the stamp pad. You want to absorb the ink but not distort the cut design. Look at your inked potato; any area that shows color, and shouldn't, should be cut away.

8. Press the inked potato onto a scrap of paper to see how the paper takes the ink. Press the potato smartly onto the paper and lift it straight up so the ink does not smear.

9. Apply the design to your paper or cards. After several imprints you will have to re-ink the potato, depending upon the effect you wish to produce. Longer printing runs will give you a softer, muted effect.

10. After 50 or so imprints, depending on the pressure you apply to the potato while printing, the edges of your design will become less sharp. Trim away the distorted edges if your design permits; if not, cut a new angel from a fresh potato.

11. If you are printing onto tissue paper, you should stamp the potato first on a paper towel to rid it of some ink.

Use this method to make place cards, greeting cards, and invitations, and to decorate paper tablecloths, napkins, and wrapping paper. When printing wrapping paper, lightly outline the surface of the box to be covered on the paper before printing. This will guide you while you are printing the angels.

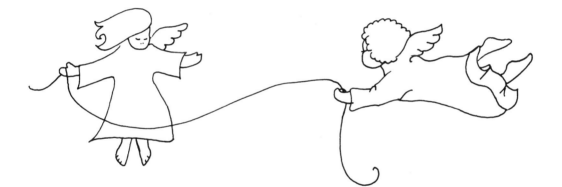

from Paradise Lost

A Seraph wing'd; six wings he wore, to shade
His lineaments Divine; the pair that clad
Each shoulder broad; came mantling o'er his breast
With regal Ornament; the middle pair
Girt like a Starry Zone his waist, and round
Skirted his loins and thighs with downy Gold
And colours dip't in Heav'n.

John Milton

Photo by Edward E. Goodwin

🌿 Angel key ring

Tools and materials

¼-inch basswood or pine, 3 inches wide by 12 inches long
a pencil
C-clamp or hand screws for holding the wood while cutting
coping saw with a fine-tooth blade
sandpaper, one square each, 150 grit and 220 grit
hand or power drill with ⅛-inch drill bit
Liquitex acrylic colors: white, red, blue; yellow or brown for hair
artists' paintbrushes, including one very fine for detail (no. 0
      or 1)
Liquitex acrylic gloss polymer medium
two metal coil key rings, 1 inch in diameter

Finished size: 4″ tall

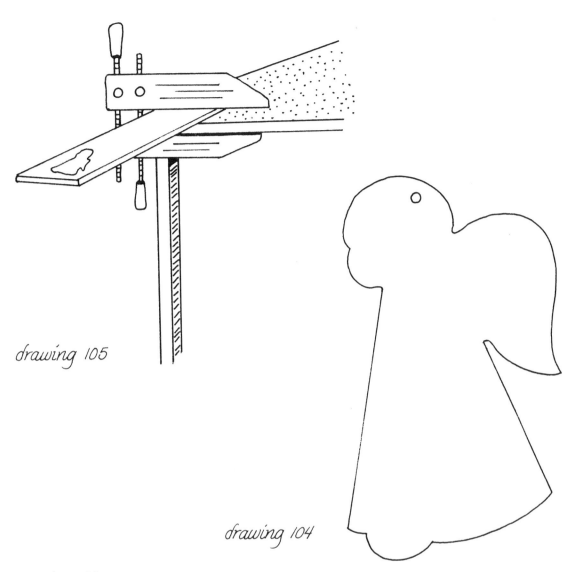

drawing 105

drawing 104

Assembly

1. Position the pattern (*see Drawing 104*) over one end of the wood, placing the angel's feet about ½ an inch from the end of the wood. The top of the wood will be the front of the angel.

2. Trace the printed pattern with a pencil, leaving a slight indentation on the wood beneath. Remove the pattern and pencil-in the indentation for a cutting guide.

3. Firmly clamp the wood to the corner of a table or workbench, with the angel on the outermost end (*see Drawing 105*). Leave at least 6 inches between the pattern and the clamp for working room with the saw.

4. Cut out the angel with a coping saw, following the cutting sequence shown in Drawing 106. You may need to reposition the clamp as you cut to allow access to the cutting lines with the saw. Cut the edges as squarely as possible. On long cut Number 5 you will have to back the saw out when you can cut no further around the wing (*point X on the cutting sequence*).

5. Sand the entire angel until it is smooth, using first the 150-grit sandpaper, and then the 220. Sand along the grain. Smooth out any saw-cut marks along the edges of the angel.

6. Drill a hole in the head for the key ring; use a ⅛-inch drill bit.

7. Paint the angel on both sides, using acrylic paint. Begin with the face and hands, extending into the dress and hair area somewhat. Next paint the wing white, again extending the white a bit into the hair and dress area. Paint the dress next, and finish with the hair. Use the small paintbrush to give detail to the hands and face, and to add flowers at the bottom of the dress.

8. Give the angel two coats of acrylic gloss polymer medium, allowing the first coat to dry completely before applying the second. Dry the angel by hanging by a thread run through the hole.

9. Attach the rings for keys.

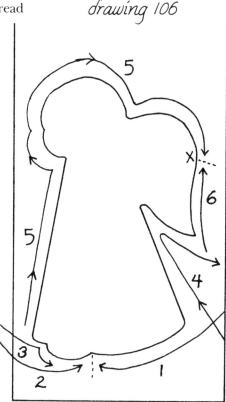

drawing 106

cutting sequence

Photo by Edward E. Goodwin

🌿 Birthday candleholders

Delight a birthday child with these candleholders, especially if the birthday falls around Christmastime. You could put the holders on an angel food or an angel-shaped cake.

Tools and materials for ten holders

thin cardboard, such as file folder or index card, at least 2 x 4 inches
a pencil
1/32-inch balsa wood, 2 inches wide by 20 inches long
X-acto knife
sandpaper, one square each, 80- or 100-, 150-, and 220-grit
Liquitex or Thalo acrylic colors, gold, bronze, red, white, and blue
1/4-inch basswood or pine, 3 inches wide by 20 inches long
C-clamp or other clamp for holding the wood secure while cutting
coping saw with a fine-tooth blade

ten round wooden toothpicks
vise (optional)
hand or electric drill with $\frac{7}{64}$-inch drill bit
Elmer's Glue-All
artists' paintbrushes, one medium (No. 3), one small (No. 1), and
    one very fine (No. 00)
Liquitex acrylic gloss polymer medium
ten wooden beads, $\frac{5}{8}$-inch in diameter, unpainted, with a $\frac{1}{4}$-inch
    hole (approximately)
ten birthday candles, $\frac{1}{4}$ inch in diameter

Finished size: 1$\frac{3}{4}$ inches, excluding candle and toothpick stem

Assembly

Wings
1. From thin cardboard, make a template for wings:
draw a circle 1$\frac{1}{2}$ inches in diameter (tracing a large spool
of thread works well), and cut out. Cut a 90-degree segment from the circle and discard it (*see Drawing 107*). Trace
the remaining form ten times onto the balsa wood, leaving
at least $\frac{1}{4}$-inch clearance between each form.
2. With a sharp X-acto knife, cut out each wing piece
carefully, making curves as smoothly as possible. With
220-grit sandpaper, smooth any rough edges.
3. Paint the wings gold or white. A 50/50 blend of
Thalo gold and Thalo bronze gives a richer effect than
straight gold. Do not use an oil-based gold, for it is not
compatible with the acrylic gloss medium which you will be
using for a final protective coating.

wing pattern guide

drawing 107

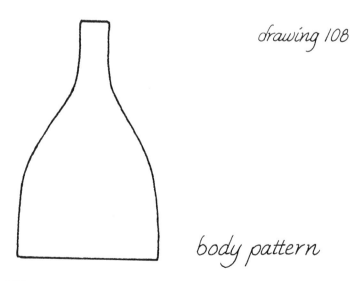

drawing 108

body pattern

drawing 109

Body

1. Trace the body pattern (*see Drawing 108*) onto thin cardboard to make a template. Cut out the template and trace it ten times onto the ¼-inch wood, beginning ¼ of an inch from one end of the length of wood and leaving ¼ of an inch between shapes.

2. Clamp the other end of the wood firmly to the corner of a table or workbench, using hand screws (wood clamps) or C-clamps.

3. Beginning with the outermost form, cut out each piece with a coping saw. Cut the pieces squarely; do not bevel the edges. (A band saw may be used instead of a coping saw.)

4. With 150-grit sandpaper, smooth the sides and bottom of the body, rounding the edges somewhat. Sand with the grain of the wood.

5. Refine the neck by running it over a piece of coarse-grit (80 or 100) sandpaper folded over an edge of a table or a block (*see Drawing 109*). Shape the neck this way until it will fit halfway into the hole on the wooden bead.

6. Sand the entire piece with 220-grit sandpaper until very smooth.

7. Sand and shape all the remaining pieces as you did the first.

Toothpick stand

1. Break ten toothpicks to a 1¼-inch length, leaving one end pointed.

2. Mark the center on the bottom edge of the body.

3. Clamp the body, upside down, in the vise or with the C-clamp. Be sure to protect the sides of soft wood from the vise/clamp with pieces of scrap wood or cardboard.

4. On the marked center, drill a hole ⅜ of an inch deep for a toothpick, using a ⁷⁄₆₄-inch drill bit. Drill a hole in the bottom center of each body piece.

5. Glue a toothpick into each hole, with the pointed end of the toothpick facing out. Wipe away any excess glue. Let the glue dry completely.

Head

1. Stand the bodies upright in a piece of Styrofoam or in the rounded side of a potato cut in half lengthwise. Leave some of the toothpick exposed.

2. Paint the bodies with a coat of acrylic gloss polymer medium. Be sure to paint the bottom of the piece and the exposed portion of the toothpick. While the medium is still wet, place the bead on the neck. Make sure the hole is upright so the candle will stand vertically.

3. When the polymer medium is dry, secure each bead/head further by dripping tiny amounts of white glue into the hole from the top of the head. Build up a small amount of glue at a time so it does not drip through any openings at the neck. The glue should not fill the hole more than halfway.

4. Let the neck joints dry completely before proceeding.

Finishing

1. Use a medium-sized brush to paint the bodies with acrylic paint. The candleholders in the picture are pink with white trim. Use a small paintbrush (No. 1) to add the trim around the angels' skirts.

2. With a fine paintbrush (No. 00), give the angels faces and hair with blue paint.

3. Insert a birthday candle in each head to check the fit. If the hole is too large reduce its diameter by building it up inside with acrylic medium and bits of sawdust. (Do not glue the candles to the holes.)

4. Glue the wing sections to the angels' backs, using Elmer's glue. Let them dry.

5. Give each entire angel and toothpick two protective coats of gloss polymer medium. Thus protected, these candleholders may be gently washed.

back

drawing 110

drawing III

🍂 Angel-shaped cake

1. Make a three-layer white cake.

2. Bake two of the layers in 8-inch cake pans; the third layer, poured to the same depth as the other two, in a one-pound coffee can.

3. Lay one of the 8-inch layers on a large platter or piece of cardboard covered with foil.

4. Cut the second 8-inch layer in half on a breadboard. Position these halves as wings beside the first 8-inch round.

5. Position the third round that was baked in the coffee can as the head of the angel.

6. Frost all with white frosting and sprinkle the wings with coconut "feathers."

7. Edge the head with yellow halo frosting.

Angel food cake

Ingredients

11 egg whites
1½ cups sugar
1 cup all-purpose flour
1 teaspoon cream of tartar
1 teaspoon vanilla

     Sift the flour once. Measure; sift four times. Sift the sugar once. Beat the egg whites a short time. Add the cream of tartar and beat the mixture to a stiff froth. Add the sugar gradually. Add the vanilla and flour. Stir gently and beat a little. Bake in a 9-inch tube pan in a 375-degree oven for 40 minutes.

1.

2.

❧ Design credits

Origami Angel, Julianna Turkevich; Claybake Angel, Julianna Turkevich; Angel Hand Puppet, Julianna Turkevich; Papier-Mâché Angel, Ursula Beau-Seigneur; Scandinavian Felt Angel, Julianna Turkevich; Cornhusk Angel, Clotilde Deschamps Guisasola of Swannanoa, North Carolina; Sachet Angel, Coffey Designs of East Greenwich, Rhode Island; Stained Glass Angel, Ann Wallace; Quilted Angel, Julianna Turkevich; Angel Cookie, Molly Lesnikowska; Gilded Cloth and Paper Angel, Julianna Turkevich; Angel in an Egg, Joan Dishman of Lynchburg, Virginia; Wooden Angel, Ruth Hawkins of Warne, North Carolina; Straw Angel, Eva Lancello; Macramé Angel, Barbara Fitzgerald; Woodland Angel, Dorothy Tresner of Asheville, North Carolina; Yarn Angel, Julianna Turkevich; Angel Sandcasting, Virginia Smith; Tissue Paper Angel, Joan Williamson; Golden Spackle Angel, Janice Hull; Wax Angels for Candlesticks, Bettyanne Twigg; Clothespin Angel, Joan Williamson; Ribbon Angel, Susan Sirkis; Leaf Angel, Susan Sirkis; Angel Puzzle, Helen Mills; Paper-Doll Angel, Julianna Turkevich; Potato Print Angels, Julianna Turkevich; Angel Key Ring, Julianna Turkevich; Birthday Candleholders, Julianna Turkevich; Angel-Shaped Cake, Norma Bridwell; Angels on Shells, Janice Belisle; and Crepe Paper and Angel Head, Elspeth.

from A Cradle Song

Sweet dreams, form a shade
O'er my lovely infant's head;
Sweet dreams of pleasant streams
By happy, silent, moony beams.

Sweet sleep, with soft down
Weave thy brows an infant crown.
Sweet sleep, Angel mild,
Hover o'er my happy child.

William Blake